COMPUTER
appreciation

Bob Dingle

HODDER AND STOUGHTON

LONDON SYDNEY AUCKLAND TORONTO

Acknowledgements

We thank the following companies and people for their permission to reproduce photographs in this book: Acornsoft, page 83 bottom left and right; P.J. Andrews, page 49 right; Apricot Computers, page 6 bottom; Baker Perkins Limited, page 26, page 27; BBC, page 6 middle; Elizabeth Bolshaw, page 35 top right, page 83 top left, right, middle; British Aerospace, page 23, page 45, page 58, page 59, page 60, page 61, page 62; British Airways, page 30; British Leyland, page 18, page 29 bottom, top; Brother, page 11 top right; CEGB page 51; Computervision, page 57; DACC, page 47 bottom right; Derek Crouch PLC, page 76; DVLC, page 16 top right; The Ford Motor Company Limited, James Galt and company, page 43; Ginn and Company Ltd., page 48; Melbourne House, page 86; Hornby Ltd, page 43; HMS Osprey, page 28; IBM page 95 J Allan Cash photolibrary, page 8; Matchbox Toys, page 43; M.C. Escher Heirs c/o Cordon Art page 91, page 99; MEMEC PLC, page 11 bottom left; NASA, Page 31 top, bottom; Novosti Press Agency, page 94; Pedigree Dolls and toys Ltd., page 43 Pelham Puppets, page 43; The Peterborough Building Society, page 15, page 78; Peterborough TVEI, page 63; Psion Limited, page 84; RS Components Ltd, page 23; Sinclair Research, page 6 top, page 82 bottom, page 83 middle, bottom, page 93 top, page 102; Spicers Limited, page 15 top; Singer Link-Miles Ltd, page 47, page 46, page 45; Spicers Limited, page 15 top; Technomatic, page 12 left; Tec Quipment International Ltd, page 22; Thorn EMI, page 39; The Times Newspapers Limited, page 20; The University of Oxford, Delegacy of Local Examinations, page 69; Humbrol Ltd., page 43.

Bob Dingle is Deputy Head Master of Orton Longueville School, Peterborough

Dingle, Bob
Computer appreciation.
1. Electronic data processing
I. Title
004   QA76

ISBN 0 340 35948 X

First printed 1986
Copyright © 1986 R. Dingle

Typeset in 10/11pt Mallard by Colset Private Ltd, Singapore.
Printed in Great Britain for Hodder and Stoughton Educational, a division of Hodder and Stoughton Ltd, Mill Road, Dunton Green, Sevenoaks, Kent TN13 2YD
by Page Bros (Norwich) Ltd.

Contents

Preface

This book is a response to the needs of teachers in the many schools that are starting computer appreciation courses. The world outside school is changing rapidly. Traditional computer studies courses and texts hold little of value for the non-specialist pupil. Most pupils will never need the level of programming or keyboard skills reached through such courses.

However, there are issues, which should be explored, that do not require programming ability but which do require a general knowledge of what computers can and cannot do. Linked to such discussions should be a chance to use computers as a learning aid. It seems that there are three distinct experiences that a school should supply through its computing curriculum.

1 A specialist computing course for the potential computer worker. (The traditional computer studies course can meet this need.)
2 A degree of computer experience through existing subjects for all pupils.
3 A chance for pupils to discover the influence that computers will have on their lives.

This book serves the third area. Teaching staff for the first two are easily identified. Computer appreciation is likely to fall to the computer studies teacher, in which case existing books are unlikely to help with the study of the widespread effects of computers on peoples' working lives and leisure time.

I have put together a book that will act as a source of information for the teacher and which will also supply a complete course for the pupil. It presents the information in a varied fashion; exercises, discussion topics, games, simulations and questions are included in the chapters and software designed to illustrate the ideas put forward in the text is also available on disc.

Bob Dingle

Dedication: For Angela, Nicholas and Emma.

Software
5¼″ disc BBC BASIC 0 340 39286 X. The disc will be available from your usual supplier.

1
Introduction

About this book

This book is about computers — the sort of computers that are in schools and in the world of work. There are many books about how computers work, how they are made and how to operate them. This book has some of these topics in it, but it takes a look at other things as well. It describes the way jobs are changing because of computers. It describes many examples of computers in use. It shows how they make things easier and how they do not solve all problems but can cause new ones.

The book has twelve chapters. Each chapter has illustrations to help you to understand the text. There are questions with every chapter, except this one. These questions need a mixture of written and spoken answers. Some are multiple choice; some need sentences to answer them; some of the questions cannot be answered by one person, but need to be discussed. As well as questions there are activities. In these you will be expected to think and talk. There is a set of computer programs to be used with the activities and questions. They simulate the real uses of computers and they will show you, first hand, the benefits that computers bring, and also some of their drawbacks.

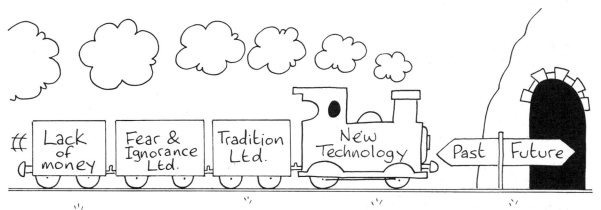

Fig. 1.1 New technology: steaming ahead!

Where are computers going to lead us?

Have a look at Fig. 1.1. This cartoon sums up how new technology is pulling all of us along. The train is a collection of coaches and trucks. The coaches, containing all of us, are being pulled along by the engine, called 'New Technology', which uses new ideas for fuel. The whole train is heading rapidly along the track into the future. At the back of the train are a number of trucks. These are slowing down the train. The trucks are called *tradition*, *lack of money*, *ignorance* and *fear*. *Tradition* means doing what has been done for years, not because this is the best thing to do but because it is the easiest; *lack of money* means that computers are expensive and companies have to find money to buy them; *ignorance* means not knowing about computers; *fear* is fear of the unknown.

The train is heading into a tunnel — no-one can see into the future. One thing is definite, the passengers will be taken into the future on this train unless they decide to jump off, which is dangerous from a fast moving train.

The cartoon illustrates some of the forces acting on people and firms. You will see the ideas shown in it several times throughout the book. When you spot one don't keep it to yourself!

A word of warning

Fig. 1.2 shows a school student's idea of how people would develop if they spent all their time in front of computers. They would have spots through lack of exercise and not washing. They would be short sighted from staring too long and too closely at a TV

Fig. 1.2 A caricature of someone who does nothing but play with a computer

screen; their fingers would develop by hitting the keys. On the other hand, these people would not need legs and so these would wither away. The pot belly would develop because of lack of exercise.

This caricature could be anyone who spends too much time in front of a micro. The lesson to learn here is 'don't get obsessed' with micros. There will be plenty of chance throughout the rest of your lives to use computers.

Finally, before you start the activity with this chapter, you must ask yourself what you should have gained after you have worked through the book. With luck and concentration you should have a much better idea of the sort of computers you will be using when you leave school. You will be able to understand why they are used in certain ways and not others. You will be able to decide what jobs you think are right for computers and which ones are best done by people.

ACTIVITY

The purpose of this activity is to show you some of the words you will meet when learning about computers. Fig. 1.3 is a games board. You can play this game with up to six people and you will need: a games board; a counter for each player; dice; 3 of each of the following tokens: a microprocessor, a power supply, a VDU, a keyboard, a memory chip, a circuit board, a disc drive, a printer, a modem, a disc, a light pen and a computer manual.

Trace the games board and enlarge it. You could stick it to a piece of cardboard for a firm base.

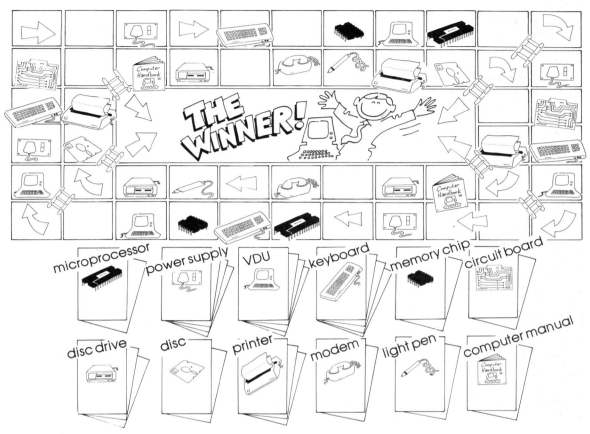

Fig. 1.3 The games board

The rules are listed below.

1 Each player has a counter.
2 Each player throws the dice in turn and moves the number of spaces shown by the dice.
3 The player to reach the middle first is the winner.
4 The board has three layers. There are 'gates' from one layer to the next at each corner of the board.
5 To pass from one layer up to the next, a player has to collect the correct tokens.
6 Tokens can be collected when a player lands on a token square.
7 The correct tokens needed to pass from layer one (the outside layer) to

layer two are: a microprocessor, a power supply, a VDU, a keyboard, a memory chip and a circuit board.
8 The correct tokens needed to pass from layer two to three are: a disc drive, a printer, a modem, a disc, a light pen and a computer manual.
9 When a player passes through a gate, his or her tokens return to the token squares they came from.
10 One player is elected as Banker before the game starts and she or he looks after the tokens as well as playing.
11 Tokens can be swapped by agreement between players.

Have fun!

2
The magic micro

Why computers?

These are comments from people in secondary schools. They show that the people who said them have little idea what computers are about. So, what *is* all the fuss about? Schools are spending money on computers. Everywhere you look there are computers; computers at the station; computers at the bank; computers at the hospital; computers in the factories; computers everywhere!

The reason for the interest in computers at school is simply that they are appearing everywhere. When you leave school, some understanding of computers will be needed no matter what you do. As an individual you need to have an idea of the power and weakness of computers in order to make good use of them. Without this knowledge the power of the computer could be used against your interests, maybe without your realising it! This book should help you to begin to understand the workings of computers and the effects they are having and will have upon your life. After working through the book you should be able to see not only how the power of computing can benefit mankind but also the dangers of such power.

Fig. 2.1 *An onion shows how difficult it is to understand computers*

Why an onion? The onion is one way of showing how difficult it will be to learn all there is to know about computers. Imagine peeling an onion. It has a skin which hides the inside and many layers underneath. Computer technology is similar. You can use computers without seeing any of the

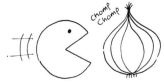

Fig. 2.2 *In this chapter we will see what's inside the 'onion'*

workings inside. Trusting in a machine is not a nice feeling. It is alright until something goes wrong. Knowing how the technology works may then be the only way to correct the mistake. Knowing how it works may tell you that there is a fault and so warn you before it's too late. If you start to ask questions about what is going on under the surface then you can peel back layer after layer and still not get to the centre of the machine. In this chapter the outer layers of the onion will be peeled back.

Fig. 2.3 *Peeling back the layers*

Getting started

Whatever make or model of computer you have, you need to take the same basic steps to make it work. First of all, the main parts of the computer must be identified.

The keyboard

Fig. 2.4, on the next page, shows some keyboards. The keyboard is used to send instructions and information to the inside of the computer. The layout of the keys is similar to that on a typewriter. The keyboard is different from a typewriter as there are several keys that do tasks other than printing letters. The ones to take care with are

These keys are used to control the computer. Pressing them can alter the way the computer behaves and may stop it altogether.

The screen

The screen, as in Fig. 2.5, is the main way that the computer tells the user what it is doing. It usually echoes the keys. In other words, a letter typed on the keyboard will appear on the screen. The screen can be a normal television set, although a better

Fig. 2.4 Keyboards for some common computers (a) the Sinclair ZX Spectrum Plus (b) the BBC micro (c) the Apricot. These keyboards all have the letters arranged in the same way to allow for fast typing. Special keys such as 'ESC' or 'STOP' are in different places on each keyboard

picture is seen using a monitor because it does not need to use as many electronic circuits as a television and the signals on it are clearer. The screen may be a colour screen giving all three primary colours, or it may be monochrome giving black and white, or black and green, only. The monitor or TV is connected to the computer by a cable which carries the signal from the computer (Fig. 2.6).

Fig. 2.5 A screen and keyboard

Fig. 2.6 This cable links the computer to a monitor

The recorder
The recorder is usually an ordinary cassette recorder but some microcomputers use a special recorder. The mechanics of these two machines are similar, but they have a different way of working. The recorder is used to save the information which is inside the computer. This information is lost when the computer is switched off unless a copy of it can be made on the tape. It can then be

loaded into the computer the next time it is needed. This system is cheap and easy to use but there are many other ways of doing the same thing, as shown later in this chapter. Although they are faster and more reliable, these ways are also more expensive. Cassette tapes, on the other hand, are very cheap and convenient.

The recorder is wired to the computer with three sets of wires. One set carries the signals from the recorder to the computer and is plugged into the earphone socket of the cassette recorder. Another set carries the signals the other way and plugs into the microphone socket so that the signal can be recorded onto tape. The last set of wires makes it possible for the computer to turn the motor of the cassette recorder on and off. This plugs into the remote socket.

Connecting up and switching on

The three main devices, the keyboard, the screen and the recorder, are connected together (as in Fig. 2.7) and mains leads are plugged into a socket. Switching on the three will result in a message on the screen telling the user something he or she already knows — the make and model of the computer. Also on the screen may be a flashing line or block which is known as the *cursor*. If a key is pressed on the keyboard, the letter should be printed at the cursor position.

People new to computers will find the output so far surprisingly dull. The computer

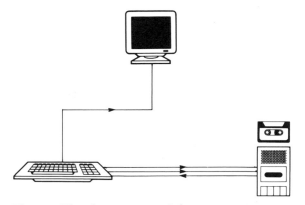

Fig. 2.7 *The three parts of the computer system are linked by using several cables that will carry electronic signals between them*

will do nothing more unless it is told what to do. We are still at the level of the onion skin. It is important now to cut the onion in two.

Hardware and software

The two parts of the onion stand for the two parts of computer technology — *hardware* and *software*. Both sides can be divided even further, as you will see.

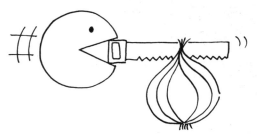

Fig. 2.8 *There are two sides to computers*

So far only the hardware parts of the computer have been mentioned. Hardware items are the solid parts of the computer that can be seen and touched. On their own they can do very little, except hum and get hot. To make the hardware perform it needs to be told what to do. The instructions or commands for the hardware come from the other half of the onion — the software, which is impossible to see. It cannot be touched or handled in the same way as the hardware. It can be heard by playing a computer cassette

Fig. 2.9 *Computers may not 'byte' but they still need to be told what to do*

through the recorder's loudspeaker, but the noise is not musical and it means nothing to human ears. We do not have the code in our heads to understand it, although when these sounds are put into the computer, it can understand the instructions and it starts to do whatever the instructions tell it to. The name given to these instructions is a *program*, shown in Fig. 2.10.

```
  1 REM PROGRAM 6-2
 10 REM  SUM1
 20  REM INITIALISE
 30   SUM=0
 40  REM FINDSUM
 50   FOR COUNTER= 1 TO 4
 60   REM PROCESS A NUMBER
 70    INPUT NUMBER
 80    SUM=SUM+NUMBER
 90   NEXT COUNTER
100  PRINT SUM
110 END
```

Fig. 2.10 A computer program in BBC BASIC

Programs for computers are like programmes for the cinema, concert hall and football matches (Fig. 2.11); they indicate what happens in chronological order. A computer program is a series of instructions, worked out by someone called the *programmer*. When followed through, these steps give the result that the programmer wanted. The next part of this chapter looks at programming in a little more detail.

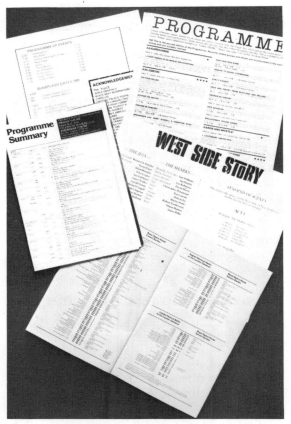

Fig. 2.11 Programmes show in which order things should happen, when they should happen and who will take part

Programming a computer

The computer can do a limited number of jobs. Its vocabulary is limited and so is the storage space. It has to look at each letter and word one at a time before it can act. It deals with one command at a time. This has a major effect on the way that computers can be used to help solve problems. There are in fact only three ways in which a computer can be set to work.

1 The computer can follow its instructions one at a time in *sequence*.
2 The computer can repeat the same sequence of instructions over and over again. This *looping* makes the machine good at jobs that people find boring.
3 The computer can compare one piece of information with another to see if they are the same. If they are different, it can tell which one is the larger. It can then *branch* to another set of instructions depending on what it finds out about the sizes of the information.

The last way means that the computer can be programmed to make decisions using the information it has been given. This makes the machine look as if it has some intelligence, but it is the programmer who has to do the hard work of setting up these branches in the program.

The basic skills needed to program have to go hand-in-hand with an idea of the problem to be computerised. The computer can perform only one action at a time in its sequence, so, before a programmer writes the program, the problem has to be broken down into a number of single steps. Take, for example, the programming of a computer to make a cup of tea. This simple task becomes surprisingly complicated when it is broken down into its simplest stages:

1 put the kettle under a running tap;
2 look at the water level in the kettle;
3 if kettle is not full go back to 1;
4 plug in the kettle;
5 switch on the kettle;
6 put tea in the teapot;
7 look at the kettle spout;
8 if the kettle is not boiling go back to 7;
9 switch off the kettle;
10 pour water into the teapot;
11 look at the water level in the teapot;
12 if the teapot is not full go back to 10.

Even these simple instructions cannot deal with all possible situations. What happens, for instance, if the kettle runs out before the teapot is full? What happens if the kettle does not work? What if the kettle is upset before it boils? The skill that the programmer has is in realising which steps are needed for the program to cover all the really possible events. The half-empty teapot and the broken kettle could be anticipated, but the spillage could not be. In the insurance business events such as spillage are known as 'acts of God'. They are not covered by the company. Programmers, like insurance companies, cannot cover every possibility.

Once the programmer has understood the problem, there are a number of techniques that can be used to 'tidy up' her or his understanding. One technique is that of *flowcharting*. This is a way of drawing out the steps using an agreed code. The point of using it is not only as an aid to programming, it also makes the programmer's thoughts clear to other people who may look at the work at a later stage. The flowchart uses boxes to represent types of action, as shown below.

A rectangle stands for an action e.g. switch on the kettle.

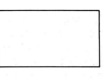

A parallelogram stands for the feeding of information into or out of the computer e.g. feed in the 'water level' information.

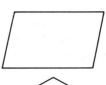

A diamond stands for a decision e.g. is the kettle boiling? If not do this; if yes do that.

A line shows the direction of flow through the chart.

A circle is used to link up parts of several flowcharts where the problem is complex.

Fig. 2.12 (on the next page) shows the instructions for making tea drawn as a flowchart. The next stage in programming is to convert these stages into 'words' or code that the computer can understand. The words used will depend on the sort of problem and the computer. There are a number of different programming languages, just like different spoken languages. The words used, and the way in which they are used, differ from one language to another. The most common language used on school computers is BASIC. The words used in BASIC are easy for people to understand and this makes programming straightforward. The disadvantage of BASIC is that once the words have been typed in, they have to be changed into a much simpler form by the computer before it can do what it has been told. This interpreting takes time. Even so, for school use the machine operates fast enough. When a faster operation is needed, say for a computer controlling a large number of machines, or giving a very detailed display, then the language used has to be directly understood by the computer without having to be interpreted, as with BASIC. Time is saved by missing out the translating stage of an interpreter. This is

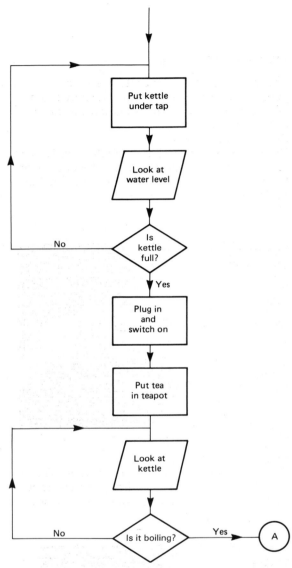

Fig. 2.12 (a) A flow chart of the instructions needed to make a cup of tea

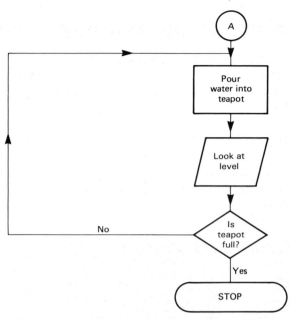

Fig. 2.12 (b) This carries on from 2.12 (a) at the circle marked A

done by using *assembly code* or *machine code* languages. There are also programs which will convert programs written in *high-level* languages, like BASIC, to *low-level* machine code. These programs are called *compilers*.

In industry, business and universities there are many specialist languages which fit the job they are to do. Some examples are given here:

dBase II is a high-level file-handling language used in commerce;
PL1 is used in research laboratories to perform difficult maths;
COBOL is used in business;
CORAL is a language used for controlling devices;
Pascal is a general-purpose high-level language used in research, industry and commerce;

The final step in programming is to test the program. During the test, situations that the programmer did not anticipate may turn up (e.g. the kettle being upset). At this stage it is difficult to make large alterations to the program, but mistakes (*bugs*) have to be corrected. This *debugging* is the last chance to put things right. Often, debugging is frustrating. The computer seems to behave as if it has a mind of its own, but in fact it is behaving in the way it has been programmed. Programmers and users find this difficult to accept. They will blame the computer even when it is their thinking and operating which are at fault.

Making the connections

The last part of this chapter will deal with some of the common pieces of hardware that can be used to make the computer more useful.

Input devices

Light pens
Light pens like the one shown in Fig. 2.13 allow the computer screen to be used as a drawing board. The picture can be altered or stored easily.

Fig. 2.13 *A light pen is more direct than the computer keys so young children and handicapped people can use it easily*

Graphics tablets
Graphics tablets are used like light pens, but to draw more complicated pictures. See Fig. 2.14.

Fig. 2.14 *This graphics tablet can be linked to a microcomputer. The pen's pressure on the pad is sensed by the computer*

Output devices

The most common output device is the printer. As typewriters work too slowly for computers, different printing mechanisms have been developed.
Dot-matrix printers
Dot-matrix printers (Fig. 2.15) print letters or pictures from a series of dots. The quality of the printing is not excellent, but it is legible and the machines work quickly.

Fig. 2.15 *A dot-matrix printer*

Daisy-wheel printers
Fig. 2.16 shows a daisy-wheel printer. These printers produce high quality print but they work more slowly than dot-matrix printers.

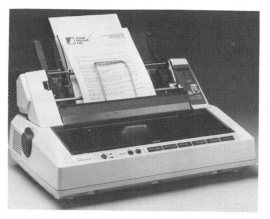

Fig. 2.16 *A daisy-wheel printer*

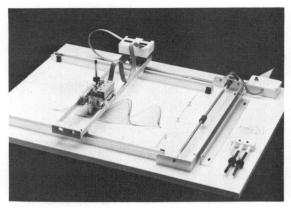

Fig. 2.17 A graph plotter

Graph plotters
Graph plotters are used to draw out and to label plans and graphs. Fig. 2.17 shows one.

Input/output devices

The most important item under this heading must be the *disc drive* shown in Fig. 2.18. Cassette recorders may be able to store information cheaply but they are not reliable or fast. A disc drive will move the information hundreds of times faster than a cassette recorder and be much more reliable. The disadvantage is the expense. A disc drive is ten times the price of a cassette recorder.

Disc drives make use of plastic discs coated with magnetic material. Just like the cassette tape, this material can have

Fig. 2.18 The inside of a disc drive

information recorded on it, erased and re-recorded. The disc, contained inside an envelope lined with soft cloth, is rotated five times a second by the drive hub. The recording head is moved across the disc as it is rotating. Like the arm on a record player, it is possible to move the head very quickly to any position on the disc. This means that the computer can find information rapidly.

Summary

This chapter has introduced some of the basic words and ideas of computing. You have learned a little about how the computer is built and you should also have some idea about the things that can be connected up to the computer from the outside world.

EXERCISES

1 Fit the following words or phrases into the sentences below:
loaded, hardware, program, flowchart, daisy-wheel, dot-matrix, light pen
   (a) Programmers use a .... to help in the design of programs.
   (b) The parts of a computer system that can be seen are known as ....
   (c) One printer that prints as well as a typewriter is a .... printer.
   (d) .... is the name given to the set of instructions that control the computer.
   (e) When programs are put into a computer they can be .... from tape.
   (f) If a picture is to be printed a .... printer can be used.
   (g) A designer may use a .... to help him or her to draw diagrams.

2 A simple job, like cleaning your teeth, is quite complicated if you try to draw it as a flowchart. Using this example, and one of your own, draw a flowchart which shows every step you take.

3 Choose the correct answers to the following questions.
   (a) Computers are becoming more widespread because:

(i) they are cheap;
(ii) they can do anything;
(iii) they work very quickly.
(b) An example of an input device is:
(i) a printer;
(ii) a light pen;
(iii) a graph plotter.
(c) Which of the following cannot be used as output devices?
(i) a disc drive;
(ii) a printer;
(iii) a cassette player.
(d) Which of the following are not used as flowchart symbols?
(i) a square;
(ii) a rectangle;
(iii) a triangle;
(iv) a diamond.

4 (a) A dot-matrix printer uses an array of dots 7 along by 9 down to make each letter or number. Using two different coloured pens draw out the letters 'T' and 'H' with the dots arranged in the same way as a printer. One colour can show where the dots do print and the other where they do not print.
(b) Go on to draw the numbers 0 to 9 in the same way.

5 A home microcomputer does not always work the first time it is plugged into the TV. Usually this is because you do not know how to connect it up properly and how to make all the necessary adjustments. Talk to your friends or other people in the class who have computers and find out what they had to do to get their computers to work. When you have done this write a list of do's and don'ts which could be given out to people who have bought their first computer.

ACTIVITIES

A1 There are many magazines for people interested in computing, for home users and for business users. Using both types of magazine, count up the number of programs that are being advertised in them and try to put these programs into sets. You should then be able to say what the most popular uses of computers are in business and in the home.

A2 Firms that make and sell computers give away a lot of posters and leaflets. Write to these firms and then make a wall display showing the variety of jobs that computers do and the different types of software.

A3 Collect a number of newspapers. Read through them carefully and highlight with a coloured pencil the articles that have the word 'computer' in them. Cut these articles out. What are the common themes in these articles?

A4 Using the newspapers from activity 'A3', cut out the advertisements for jobs involving computers. Make a list of the different types of job, the qualifications needed, the pay and the suggested age of the applicants.

A5 The sleeve for a floppy disc looks like Fig. 2.19. The warning circles show the conditions for use. Can you tell what they mean? Can you also explain why these conditions need to be followed?

Fig. 2.19 The sleeve of a floppy disc

3
Switching to computers: data processing and other applications

This chapter does not go into the details of how data processing or robotics work. There are many other excellent books that explain the ins and outs of data processing. G.M. Croft's book *Computer Studies A Practical Approach* (Hodder and Stoughton) is one worth looking at. There is a chapter on robots in this book which explains how they work.

This chapter looks instead at some companies and factories that have been computerised. It describes why computers

have to be used. It looks at the way the computer has changed the jobs of working people. It also describes examples where computers are not being used even though they would bring about improvements. For each example a number of questions are asked. Why were computers needed? What jobs do the computers do? What sort of computers were used? What effects were there on people? Was the introduction a success? First of all, a little history.

The coming of the computer

Data processing means taking information made up of letters and figures, changing it according to certain rules and sending the new information to a place where it is used. Until the 1960s this was done using manual methods on paper, although a few pieces of machinery helped to move the paper around (Fig. 3.1). Large stores, for example, had overhead wires that carried tins of money from the shop floor to the accounts office. In some, pneumatic pipes were used to move the paper around. This method is being re-introduced in some places, like in Fig. 3.2, because it is very secure.

As computers became more reliable, the largest firms started to use them to help with

moving and organising information. This chapter will describe some of the data processing applications. The examples have not been chosen to show data processing at its best, they show instead the benefits and problems of new technology. They show how computers have changed peoples' jobs and how computers have changed companies' ways of working.

Swansea — a new start

In the 1960s there was a rapid increase in car ownership. Every car and its driver had to be licensed at one of the county licensing centres. As more applications for licences

Fig. 3.1 *All of these were used in offices to help with paperwork. They are still seen in some offices*

were made, these 183 centres became unable to cope with the work. Fig. 3.3 shows some of the licence forms which are used.

Not only was the county-based licensing system overloaded, but it was inefficient too. If people moved to a new county, all their licensing information had to be transferred. Often it was possible for someone to lose his or her licence in one county, and to reapply somewhere else and receive a new licence. It was not easy to trace information about individual licences.

In 1969 a large computer centre was built at Swansea in Wales. This centre was designed to replace the 183 county licensing centres and it took control of all vehicle and driver licensing. The centre is called the Driver and Vehicle Licensing Centre (DVLC);

Fig. 3.2 *These building society offices are fitted with an air tube system that carries money and paper to and from the cashiers. This system makes the whole office more open and friendly as well as speeding up the business of paying in and taking out money*

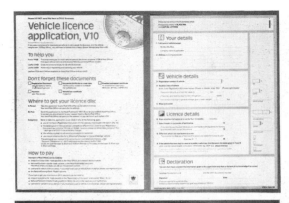

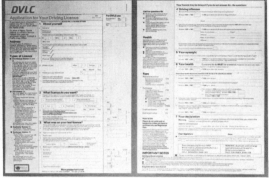

Fig. 3.3 *The information on these forms is passed to Swansea. There it is entered onto a computer file. This file then sends out reminders when licences have to be renewed*

Fig. 3.4 *The DVLC*

Fig. 3.4 shows the outside of it. It now holds all the licensing records in the country on a series of computer files which can be very easily updated and checked.

The centre has had some problems over the years but there is no doubt that it is much more efficient than the original system.

Places that changed to computers

Swansea was built from scratch. It had new buildings, new people working in it, and new machines. Like a new school it had everything going for it. Other places are not so lucky.

British Airways

Swansea deals with a large amount of information — 60 million records. This service needs 150 computer staff to make it work. The British Airways computing department, on the other hand, is nearly five times bigger. Over 700 computer experts work for it. Mention airlines to a computer studies teacher and she or he will think of the computer booking system in Fig. 3.5, but this is only a small part of the vast computing power that keeps British Airways going.

Why does an airline need computers?
The simple answer is that a lot of people fly but there is more to the answer than this.

Before every flight takes off a lot of arrangements have to be made. Computers can deal with the 12 million or so tickets used every year, the 2 million bookings held at any one time, and the details of the 35,000 employees of British Airways. This large amount of information could be held manually but, as was the case with the DVLC, a manual system would be slow and inaccurate. In a business like an airline, fast communication is needed. Information needs to be sent to other airports in this country and abroad. Computers can do this. They can also be programmed to double check

Fig. 3.5 An airline booking counter has several computer terminals on it. There is a much greater use for computers in airlines than this application

information given to them and so to eliminate human error.

There is another reason why British Airways started to use computers. The cost of computers has fallen since 1965 when British Airways started to use them. This meant that computers could be used to do more jobs. Every time a computer was used, the amount of work done by the company increased. This is called *increased productivity*. With computers, British Airways could do more business employing the same number of people, or the same amount of business with fewer people employed. Infact, a good estimate is that airlines generally have chosen a situation between these two options; to do a third as much work again with fewer workers by using computers. It is not, however, a free

choice. Airlines that did not use computers to increase their productivity (and lose some jobs) went out of business. The choice facing the airlines since the mid '60s has been to computerise or to go bust. This pattern will be seen again in this chapter.

How did the introduction of the British Airways computers affect people?

British Airways used computers to make the company more efficient. Like the DVLC they would not have been able to deal with the increase in travellers without computers. For members of the public it means that travelling by plane has become less expensive and so available to more people.

The effect of this computerisation on people working for British Airways is more difficult to measure. Those people who have worked for British Airways ever since the mid-sixties have had to learn new skills to be able to work with the computers. This has meant that they have had to be retrained. Retraining is another common problem when computers are introduced.

British Leyland

During the 1970s, competition from foreign companies meant that British cars were considered expensive and unreliable. To stay in business, British car manufacturers had to improve the efficiency and quality of their work.

On the original production lines, a car was built in stages as it moved along the line. A worker at each stage was responsible for doing one job, such as fitting a door or a steering wheel. Each person was skilled to work on only one part of the assembly line. This system was inefficient for two reasons. A problem at any point along the line held up work throughout that line. This itself meant that problems in production were expensive and inspectors were necessary to supervise the smooth running of each line. The second problem was that if there was no work along one part of an assembly line, it was impossible to transfer the workers to do another job elsewhere.

British Leyland (BL) overcame both these problems when they installed a computer system and new factory machines. The production lines are now broken down into smaller units called *empires*. Each empire is run by a foreman, and the people working in the empire can do a number of different jobs. This means that stoppages along the production line do not stop production completely, and the manpower can be moved around the factory to wherever there are jobs to be done.

BL have introduced automatic testing machines to check the quality of the car bodies. There is now also a central stock-control computer which efficiently handles stock moving into and out of the warehouse. Goods are checked into the warehouse on a wooden tray (pallet) marked with a *bar code* (like those found on supermarket goods). A light sensitive pen is used to read the code (Fig. 3.6), and the information is transferred to the central computer which produces the bills and receipts for the goods. The computer also directs an automatic crane to store the pallet in the right place. Fork lift trucks are used to collect the pallet when it is taken out of the warehouse. Eventually, these trucks will be replaced by automatic robot trucks. This system is extremely fast; it saves BL a lot of money and time.

What was the cost?

The introduction of computer technology had a severe effect on the staff at BL. Initially, about 10 000 jobs were lost, and the people remaining had to change the way they worked. Retraining so many people cost a lot of money. The total cost of the computerisation at BL was about double that of the British Airways Conversion.

Fig. 3.6 A computer-linked light pen records pallet contents in the Metro automated body pallet store

Places that have not gone all the way

British Airways and British Leyland had to computerise to survive. If they had not started to use computers and improved their service then foreign companies would have taken away their business. Where there is less competition there is, perhaps, less need to computerise.

ACTIVITY

Read the following passage:

Smallville is a small town near London. The largest employer is a firm, called Green's Plastics, that manufactures plastic goods like baby baths and yoghurt pots. The firm is going through a difficult time; cheap imports are undercutting its goods and so the sales of its products are going down. A few staff have already lost their jobs. The sales manager, Mr Brown, is possibly the next person to go since he is responsible for sales. The owner, Mr Green, has a go-ahead niece, Jane Red, who runs his computer department. She has already computerised the accounts department with the loss of 10% of the workforce there and she has a plan to bring in computer-controlled moulding machines and computer-controlled warehouse equipment. The people opposed to this are the two workers' representatives, Mr. Blue and Mrs. Baggins, both of whom have worked for the company for more than ten years. On their side also is the firm's accountant, Mr. Money. He cannot see how the venture will pay for itself.

In groups of seven decide who is going to play which of the characters and who is going to make notes. On paper, write down what you can about the character you are going to play, what the person thinks of computers, where her or his loyalties lie, what he or she is frightened of etc. When you are ready, imagine you are seated around the board table of Green's Plastics. You are there to decide whether to go for Jane's idea or not. After ten minutes the note-taker will report your decision to the rest of the class.

Mr Brown
(sales manager)

Mr Green
(the owner)

Jane Red
(computer manager)

Mr Money
(the accountant)

Mr Blue
(a worker)

Mr Baggins
(a worker)

Fig. 3.7 *The members of Green's Plastics*

The national newspapers

Britain's newspaper industry is centred around Fleet Street in London. Every night, giant presses print the millions of newspapers that will be read at breakfast the next morning. It is a high pressure business which is only partly computerised so far.

When a story has been typed out by a journalist and approved by the editor, it is passed to the printers and converted into metal plates mounted on the drums of the presses. This used to be done by retyping the story on a *typesetting machine* which is like a huge typewriter. The machine casts a letter in metal every time a key is pressed; the metal letters are then assembled onto plates and mounted on drums for printing. This is not very efficient. The story has to be typed twice so there is twice the possibility of mistakes.

Newspaper owners have tried to replace this process by something more up-to-date. New technology can make newspaper production much faster and more efficient. Stories are typed by journalists on to wordprocessors linked directly to platemaking machines. The plates are then transferred to the press. This cuts out several stages in the printing process. Fewer people are employed, so the newspaper is cheaper to run and there are likely to be fewer mistakes. The time between the story breaking and the newspaper appearing is also reduced. This time has always been the way in which the success of a newspaper has been measured.

Why are national newspapers not using new technology?

It is not clear why national newspapers are not using new technology. It may be because of bad planning, insufficient training, or the unions. The print unions are very powerful and they protect their members' rights, especially in issues involving possible job losses. The introduction of computers would mean job loss and retraining for a large number of printers. The national newspaper unions have so far been successful in resisting computerisation.

At *The Times* newspaper a compromise has been reached. Journalists type their stories and printers retype them on to wordprocessors which allow the printers to arrange the articles as they choose on the newspaper page. A printed copy of the story is then produced and 'pasted-up' on a board, shown in Fig. 3.8. The finished board is photographed and the printing plates are made from the photograph negative.

As you can see from these examples, the problems faced by printers and managers introducing new technology are human problems as much as technical problems.

Fig. 3.8 This printer is putting together a page of a newspaper. The story that he is working on was typed into a computer on a 'typesetting wordprocessor'. When the story comes out of the computer printer it is stuck onto a board. The completed board is made into a plate which fits onto the presses

EXERCISES

1 Which of the following best describes data processing?
- (a) processing data;
- (b) writing on paper;
- (c) sending out information;
- (d) taking in information;
- (e) working with information.

2 Which of the following describe why the DVLC was set up?
- (a) Swansea needed more jobs;
- (b) there were a lot of loopholes in the old system;
- (c) the old system used a lot of paper;
- (d) the old system could no longer cope;
- (e) there were a lot of drivers.

3 Which of the following things did British Leyland decide to do to help it to make better cars?
- (a) reduce the number of workers;
- (b) stop holidays;
- (c) pay more money;
- (d) retrain workers;
- (e) use new technology.

4 Why did British Leyland make all the changes?
- (a) they were fed up with their cars;
- (b) they were losing money;
- (c) they were losing jobs;
- (d) they were told to by the workers;
- (e) they felt like it.

5 Which of the following are true? The warehouse at British Leyland has:
- (a) no workers;
- (b) no robots;
- (c) fork lift trucks;
- (d) bar codes;
- (e) cars.

6 When new technology is being put into places which of the following problems is the most difficult to solve?
- (a) who makes the tea;
- (b) who loses his or her job first;
- (c) which computer to use;
- (d) where the power socket is;
- (e) which programs to use.

TOPICS FOR DISCUSSION

D1 You are the owner of a national newspaper and you want to make more money. Which of the following things would you do?
- (a) Sack all the printers and use robots?
- (b) Move out of London and use new printers?
- (c) Sit down and talk with the printers?
- (d) Sell the newspaper and live off the money?
- (e) Invent another solution?

D2 You are talking to the manager of a company that started to use computers two years ago. Which of the following questions tells you the most about the way in which a company introduced new technology?
- (a) What profit did you make last year?
- (b) How many people lost their jobs last year?
- (c) How much did the computer cost?
- (d) Who helped you to get the new technology working?
- (e) How much do you get paid?

D3 What was the choice facing British Airways?
- (a) whether to use computers or manual methods;
- (b) whether to use more planes or more computers;
- (c) whether to use computers or to go out of business;
- (d) whether to use computers instead of aeroplanes;
- (e) whether to use computers or to go on without any changes.

D4 Which of the following best describes 'The Times' newspaper?
- (a) It is based in Fleet Street;
- (b) It uses new technology;
- (c) It uses old technology;
- (d) (b) and (c);
- (e) (a), (b) and (c).

4
Computers in control

In 1818 Mary Shelley, the wife of Percy Shelley the poet, published a book. The story was about a young scientist, called Frankenstein, who put together a creature and brought it to life. The creature turned on the scientist and his relatives and eventually they all died. The creature then wandered off into the wilderness. This novel was a best-seller, and there can be few of you who have not heard of Frankenstein.

The word *robot* comes from a different writer. In 1921 Karel Capek wrote a play called 'R.U.R.', which stood for 'Rossum's Universal Robot'. The word robot came from the Czech word meaning 'worker'. The fear that many people now have is that robot-like creatures, put together by scientists, will one day turn on mankind and 'take over' just as Frankenstein's creature did in Mary Shelley's story. There are several other stories that have this same idea of the monster turning on his or her maker. One of them is Arthur C. Clarke's '2001'. In this story a spaceship on its way to Jupiter is controlled by a computer called HAL. The computer becomes confused by various instructions it had been given before it left Earth. It decides that the men on board are no longer needed and are a threat to the mission it has been sent on. It proceeds to kill them one by one. The truth is not as frightening. This chapter explains how near we are to building a robot.

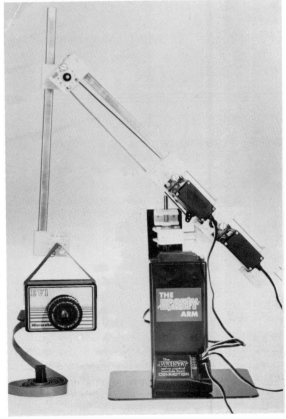

Fig. 4.1 'The Beasty!' This robot can move things around with its computer-controlled arm

Designing a robot

Fig. 4.1 shows a robot. A robot must be able to sense what is around it, to understand what it 'sees' and to change its surroundings. There are three items which a robot must have in order to do these activities.

1 Sensors — these, like our ears, eyes, nose, taste-buds and finger-tips, give the robot a sense of the world around.
2 Limbs — with some form of arm the robot can alter the world around it.
3 A 'brain' — a computer with a suitable program is the closest that we can get to an artificial brain, so that the robot can understand the information from its sensors.

Fig. 4.3 A pressure sensor

Fig. 4.4 A smoke and gas detector

Fig. 4.5 A hall probe. This unit senses magnetic fields

Fig. 4.2 Life can be tough for a robot!

We will now look at these three items in more detail.

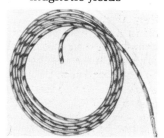

Fig. 4.6
A thermocouple. This probe senses temperature

Sensors

The following figures show some sensors that are connected to computers.

These six examples are just a few of the many sensors that are being connected to computers. Some of them do not correspond to any of our senses. A robot equipped with these sensors would be able to 'see' things around it that humans would not be aware of. Which ones are they?

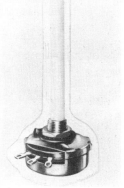

Fig. 4.7
A potentiometer. This is used to sense position

Fig. 4.8
A gyroscope assembly from an autopilot. This is used to sense changes of direction

Limbs

Computers have been linked to 'limbs' only recently, because the electronic components needed to do this are now cheap enough.

There are as many sorts of control items as there are sensors. A few of them are shown in Fig. 4.9. With these control devices the computer can turn on and off the power needed to move things around.

Fig. 4.9 Various control items. From the top, clockwise, they are: a relay, stepper motor, thyristor and a power transistor

The computer — a robot brain

Fig. 4.10

The third part of our design needs a computer. The robot 'brain' will make use of all of the power of the computer to memorise, calculate, make choices and repeat what it is doing. The sensors have to be connected to the computer and its software to make sense of their signals. The computer will also need to be connected to control devices.

The connections to the input sensors and the output control devices, shown in Fig. 4.11, are called *ports*. You will find the ports at the back of the microcomputer and/or underneath the computer. There may be input and output devices connected to your computer — disc drives and printers for instance.

Two types of port are used in microcomputers — the *analogue port* and the *digital port*.

Fig. 4.11 The ports at the back of a BBC microcomputer

These two types of port are the link (*interface*) between the computer and the outside world. Fig. 4.12 shows a simple link-up between the three items: a photocell is connected to the input, and a light source is connected to the output. A very simple computer program is now needed to make the three items act together in a useful way.

Suppose the purpose of this simple set-up is to keep the amount of light in a room the same, no matter what the time of day or night it is. The simple program in the computer would take the number from the analogue port, compare this number with the ideal number (the number standing for the ideal lighting level) and act on what it found. If the number from the sensor was too high, the computer would turn down the light until the number from the sensor was the same as the ideal number. A simple flowchart for this action is shown in Fig. 4.13. Another way of

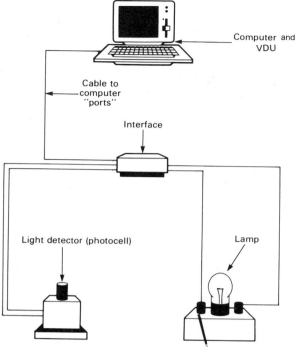

Fig. 4.12 *A simple light-control system*

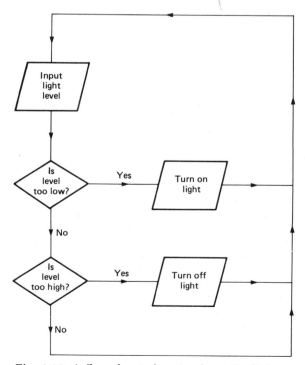

Fig. 4.13 *A flowchart showing how the light-control system works*

drawing the system, rather than using a flowchart, is to use a block diagram as in Fig. 4.14. All control systems use an idea which is missing from this diagram.

Fig. 4.14 *A block diagram of the light-control system*

The photocell is linked to the light in TWO ways, not just one. The obvious way is through the computer, but less obvious is the fact that the sensor will sense not only the sunlight but also the light produced by the light source. Fig. 4.14 should therefore be drawn like Fig. 4.15. The photocell is linked to the light by the rays which the light itself gives off.

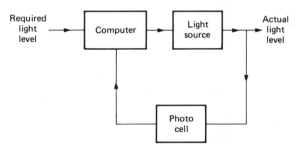

Fig. 4.15 *A block diagram of the light-control system including the feedback path*

The line joining the output device to the input of the computer stands for a *feedback* path. In our case, this path is made by rays of light from the light source falling on the sensor. In other places it may be built-in deliberately. For example, a potentiometer is placed on a robot arm to feed back information on the actual position of the arm to the computer. This actual position can then be compared with the ideal position and the computer instructs the arm to move to correct any errors. This sort of feedback is called *negative feedback*. It takes away mistakes.

Although the idea of feedback is not too difficult, designing real control systems is difficult. There are many factors to take into account and the mathematics needed to work out the answers is complicated. This sort of design work is called *systems design*.

ACTIVITIES

A1 Robot An idea of the problems
involved in systems design and controlling
devices can be seen using the program
called **Robot** which accompanies this
book. The problem you have to solve is
how to steer a robot from its starting point
at the top left-hand corner of the screen to
the finishing point at the bottom right-hand
corner of the screen in as short a time as
possible (see Fig. 4.16). It can be steered
in four directions, north, south, east and
west and it must not hit the sides of the
screen (roughly 1000 units across). To
make life more complicated there are
obstacles in the form of coloured
rectangles in its way. These represent the
machines in the factory and if the robot
hits these, it is destroyed. The person
controlling the robot has to set up a series
of commands telling the robot which
direction to go in and how far to go. The
fastest time is the winner and the program
has been written so that you get only one
attempt. If the robot is crashed then the
program of commands has to be entered
again. It will become obvious very quickly
to those using the program that a piece of
paper and a pencil are needed for
success.

This programming is similar to that
involved in the operation of a computer-
controlled milling machine (which cuts
metal) shown in Fig. 4.17. The operator has
to set up the instructions before a single
piece is made. This process will probably
take more time than making a single
piece. However, once the instructions
have been written correctly, then the
machine will turn out pieces much faster
than a manual machine. In some
instances, where the pieces are complex
(such as that in Fig. 4.18) then the only
economic way to make them is to use a
computer-controlled device.

A2 Another demonstration of the
problems of control can be done without
a computer. This demonstration needs two
people to work together using paper with
a cross in the middle and a pencil. The
two people will be called **A** and **B. A**
should first of all be blindfolded and given

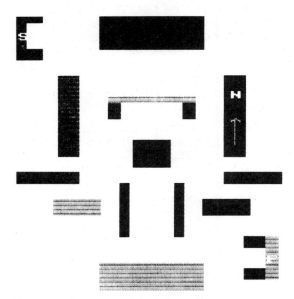

Fig. 4.16 A screen dump from the program
'Robot'

Fig. 4.17 This computer-controlled milling
machine works three times faster than
manual machines. The table in the middle has
the job on it. The operator works on the right.
On the left, is the selection of tools that the
machine can use.

the pencil and paper. **B** will try to get **A** to draw a line from the bottom left of the paper to the cross on the paper using only the commands: stop; up; left; down; right. Try the problem several times and then change over so that **B** is blindfolded and **A** gives the instructions.

Several ideas should come out of this activity.

1 The first few times each person gets near the target there will be **overshoot** (the person will go beyond the target).
£ The two people learn from their experiences, and the control improves as they repeat the activity.

Overshoot and **hunting** for the target are sometimes seen in poorly designed control systems. They are corrected by adding more feedback to the system or by making the system inefficient. In a computer control system, the program itself can be changed to stop these mistakes happening.

Learning from experience is an important quality for any robot system to have. Just how it is included is best left to the chapter on artificial intelligence. At the moment, most robots lack the ability to learn from their experiences. The operator has to make up for this and the examples which follow in this chapter show how.

Fig. 4.18 *Complex pieces of metal that have been cut by a computer controlled milling machine*

Robots in action

Robots in war

During the Second World War a great deal of progress took place in the design of computing equipment. The link between computing, control and robotics and the building of war machines is still strong. It costs a lot of money to develop computer systems; the software has to be written; the computers have to be built; and the machines which they control have to be put together. The cost of developing these systems can sometimes only be met from the large amounts of money given to defence. In order to do their jobs, the armed forces of one country have to be as advanced or more advanced than those of other countries. They have to respond to attack quickly and accurately, so they must be equipped with sensing devices, such as radar, and weapons to act as 'limbs'. The speed of warfare today has made computers essential to the link between sensors, weapons and fire-control (the term used to describe the way in which weapons are selected, aimed and fired). The result is a computerised weapon system which is almost 'robot'.

Figures 4.19, 4.20 and 4.21 show the components which make up this 'robot' weapon system, and Figure 4.22 shows the electronic systems that help the flight crew in a fighter plane.

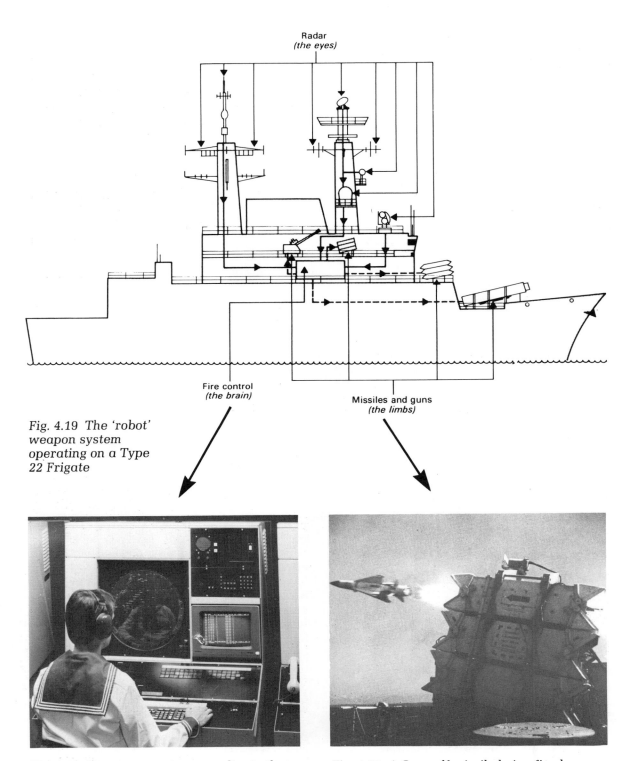

Radar
(the eyes)

Fire control
(the brain)

Missiles and guns
(the limbs)

Fig. 4.19 The 'robot'
weapon system
operating on a Type
22 Frigate

Fig. 4.20 Human operators coordinate the
'weapon' system

Fig. 4.21 A Seawolf missile being fired

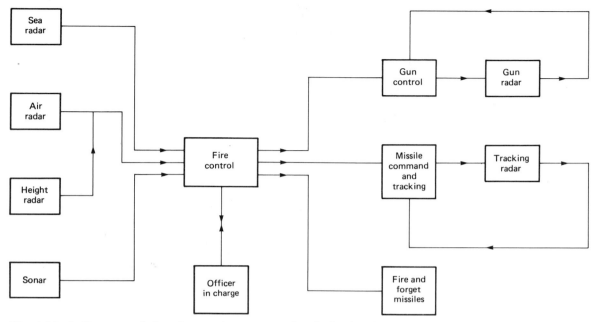

Fig. 4.22 A diagram of the electronic systems that help the flight crew in a fighter plane

Robots in the factory

Robots are gradually taking over jobs previously done by people on the shop floor. BL use robots on their Mini Metro production line, for example in Automatic Body Framing (ABF), Fig. 4.23. This is where various panels are brought together and welded to make the car body shell, as shown in Fig. 4.24. There are 28 robots on the ABF lines. Each one is programmed to repeat the same operation over and over again. Some of the robots even move around the car as they work.

This has been a big saving for BL. There are now only 38 people employed on the ABF lines to service the robots. The cost of buying, running and maintaining the robots is much less than the cost of employing the 138 people necessary to run an equivalent manual department.

Robots are used in other parts of the Mini Metro plant. They save money and time (they

Fig. 4.23 These car bodies are being moved by computer-controlled machines.

never go on strike!), but they require human operators to maintain them and to program them. For example, robots cannot pick up materials left in the wrong place or dropped.

Fig. 4.24 *One of the two synchronised robot welding lines for the Mini Metro*

Robots in the sky

To fly a civil airliner, the pilot must control various flaps and moving surfaces on its wings. Many other systems such as the engines, radar, fuel, wheels etc. must also be monitored and co-ordinated. The automatic pilot (or autopilot) was developed early on in the history of civil flying to release the pilot completely from the task of keeping the aircraft flying straight and level. It is now one of a number of electronic systems used to assist the flight crew. Many of these systems are now linked by several central computers which can keep the pilot informed and take over his job completely. The pilot now simply checks that the automatic systems are behaving (Fig. 4.25).

The description of a robot at the start of this chapter can be applied to the automatic systems in an aircraft. There are sensors (such as radar for navigation and thermocouples to measure engine temperatures), there are limbs (the devices which control the systems moving the aircraft control surfaces) and the central computer acts as a brain.

Robot systems can be made to control the whole of a normal flight, from take-off to

Fig. 4.25 *This photo of a Trident autolanding in poor visibility shows how sophisticated robots in the sky have become*

landing. They can make sure that the engines are used at their most economical setting throughout the flight. They can navigate from one point to the next according to a preset plan. They can land the aircraft without any help from the pilot at all.

Fig. 4.26 *The Viking spacecraft was controlled by its own robot systems. It was too far from Earth to be controlled by radio systems alone*

Robots in space

In 1976 the United States soft-landed two robots on the surface of Mars. The Viking spacecraft, shown in Fig. 4.26, touched down in a similar way to the Apollo lunar modules. The spacecraft had vertical rocket motors to alter the speed of descent. These motors were controlled by an on-board computer which was fed with information about the height and speed of the spacecraft from radio altimeters and gyroscopes. This part of the spacecraft control was very similar to the automatic control of missiles.

Having landed, the Viking robots then started to experiment on the ground around their base (Fig. 4.27). Soil was collected by a powered collector head or arm, and transferred for testing to an automatic laboratory or *bio-lab* in the body of the spacecraft. The tests showed that there was no life in the soil.

The programmed instructions for these tests had been placed in the computer by scientists at the Californian control centre. They were a complex series of instructions which allowed the robot to carry on with the task of analysis without needing direct human control. At its closest, Mars is 36 million miles from Earth. As radio waves take over three minutes to travel that distance, the control of the robot arm and the experiments inside the bio-lab had to be under close computer control.

Fig. 4.27 *This is the surface of Mars. The Viking spacecraft used a robot arm to lift samples from this surface into its robot laboratory*

ACTIVITIES

In many ordinary tasks we depend on feedback. These two activities will show you the effects of changing the feedback.

A1 Try to direct a blindfolded friend, using as few words as possible, to pin the tail on a paper donkey. When you can do this easily, try to do it again but instead of saying a command, whisper it to someone else. This person then gives your friend the command.

You are now putting a delay into the system. What effect does this delay have on the quality of the control? Does it alter the time that your friend takes to find the right place for the tail. Is there overshoot or hunting? If your friend moves more slowly is control better again?

A2 You can alter the feedback path between your voice-box and your brain by using a tape recorder. For this activity you need a 'three head' tape recorder, a microphone and headphones. An ordinary tape recorder will not work. You will probably find that the music department has a 'three head' machine. The person who is going to try the experiment wears the headphones and has to speak into the microphone. The microphone is plugged into the tape recorder and the headphones are used to monitor from the tape. Set the machine recording and the person wearing the headphones should start speaking. This person will hear what has been said a little time after having said it. This is because the microphone signal is placed onto the tape by one head and monitored by another head some distance from the first head. A slight delay of about one second results. This activity reduces even the most talkative person to grunts.

Your brain is accustomed to receiving feedback from your speech by hearing your own voice. It then uses a series of patterns as a guide to alter the shape of your voice box in order to correct any mistakes in the sounds which you are making. By first passing the sounds from

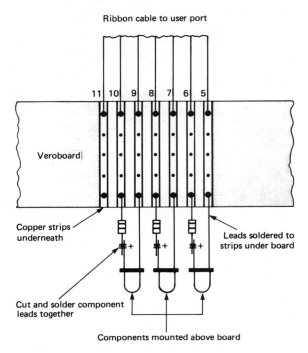

Ribbon cable to user port

Veroboard

Copper strips underneath

Leads soldered to strips under board

Cut and solder component leads together

Components mounted above board

Approximate cost is 50p + cost of ribbon cable and IDC connector

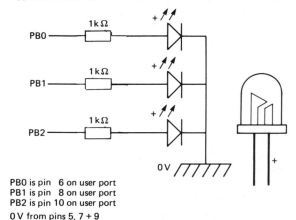

PB0 is pin 6 on user port
PB1 is pin 8 on user port
PB2 is pin 10 on user port
0 V from pins 5, 7 + 9

Fig. 4.28 A circuit to demonstrate a simple example of control (see A4)

your voice through a tape-recorder, the feedback to your voice is delayed and the signals which your brain receives are altered. The brain tries to correct the mistakes, but unfortunately, the patterns which it has do not work in this new situation.

A3 Robot design can be fun even if the models built are only mock-ups. Use what has been said in this chapter about sensors, limbs and computers to design robots for the following tasks. The designs should be on paper first of all. Once they have been talked through they could be built out of cardboard etc.

(a) An undersea robot to service oil rigs.
(b) A robot to do the housework.
(c) A robot to explore caves.
(d) A robot which will help an old person.
(e) A robot to perform on a musical instrument.

A4 Information about the way in which computers are used by the armed forces and the sort of people who use them can be obtained from any Army, RAF or RN Careers Information Centre. The posters produced by the services provide a lot of material for displays.

A5 The simplest possible example of control using the BBC computer involves the user port, three 1000 ohm resistors, three small LEDs (Light Emitting Diodes) and a cable to plug into the user port. Wire the LEDs up on a small piece of circuitboard as shown in Fig. 4.28. Take care to put in the LEDs the right way round. Type in the following simple program:

```
10REM Program to demonstrate
control of lights
20?&FE62=&FF: REM set the user
port to output
30REPEAT: REM start of loop
40A$=INKEY$(0): REM test for a
key press
50IF A$="1" PROClight(1)
60IF A$="2" PROClight(2)
70IF A$="3" PROClight(4)
80UNTIL FALSE: REM end of loop
90END
100DEFPROClight(number):REM this
part turns on/off the light
110?&FE60=0
120?&FE60=number:REM turn on
the correct light
130t=TIME:REPEAT UNTIL TIME>t+250
:REM keep light on for 2.5 seconds
140ENDPROC
```

This program sets up the computer so that pressing the number keys 1, 2, or 3 turns on the LEDs in that order. Those of you who have studied programming may be able to alter the program so that the lights are lit in different ways.

EXERCISES

1 Draw block diagrams for the following activities. On the diagrams mark the sensors, computing parts, limbs and feedback paths:—

(a) human speech system;
(b) driving a car;
(c) riding a bicycle;
(d) playing snooker;
(e) buying an LP;
(f) the telephone system;
(g) a living plant;

2 Write out a set of instructions for making a bed. The instructions must be as simple as possible. You can put questions in the instructions but they must be simple enough to be answered by only 'yes' or 'no'.

3 Read the following list of jobs: teacher; typist; dentist; nurse; housewife; bank clerk; dustman; postman; spot welder; brick-layer; carpenter; draughtsman. Write down each job, and next to it write down what is needed to build a robot which would replace the human being who does the job at the moment. Take care to name the sort of sensors and limbs required. Also, guess how easy it would be to program the robot. Are there some jobs which can be done by robots? Are some jobs never going to be done by robots? If so, what is special about those jobs? Do they need skills with which a robot could never be programmed?

4 Choose from the following list the words that fit these sentences.
Photocell; thermocouple; proximity sensor; smoke detector; strain gauge; potentiometer; gyroscope; lamp; stepping

motor; relay.

(a) A .... converts position into an electrical signal.

(b) The central item in a modern navigation system is a ....

(c) Fire alarms sometimes have ....

(d) An electrical weighing machine uses .... to convert weight into an electrical signal.

(e) A street light uses a .... as well as a timer so that it comes on at the best time.

(f) .... are found in family cars as well as in robot systems.

5 Disabled people can be helped a lot by the robot technology which you have read about in this chapter. Describe how you would use the technology to help a person with a disability.

TOPICS FOR DISCUSSION

D1 Isaac Asimov is a well known writer of science fiction. He has suggested that when robots reach the stage of being selfprogramming and selfpropelled they should obey three basic laws. Before you read the next part try to make up three laws which you would program robots to obey.

The three laws which Asimov thought of were as follows.

Law 1 A robot must not harm a human or allow a human to come to harm.

Law 2 A robot must obey orders given to it by humans except when they conflict with law 1.

Law 3 A robot must protect itself as long as its protection does not conflict with the first two laws.

Law 1 is a way of avoiding the monsters of popular fiction — the robot running wild. Why are laws 2 and 3 needed?

D2 The following text is a shortened version of part of Douglas Adams's 'The Hitch-Hikers Guide to the Galaxy'

'Hello'

'Hello lift'

'I am to be your elevator for this trip to the floor of your choice. If you enjoy your ride, which will be swift and pleasurable, then you may care to enjoy some of the other elevators which have recently been installed.'

'Yeh, what else do you do besides talk?'

'I go up or down'

'Good, we're going up'

'Or down!'

'OK, up please'

'Down's very nice'

'Good, now will you take us up!'

'May I ask whether you've considered all the possibilities down might offer you?'

'Like what?'

'Well there's the basement, the micro files, the heating system . . . . nothing particularly exciting, I'll admit, but they are alternative possibilities'

'What's the matter with the thing?'

'It doesn't want to go up, I think its afraid'

'Of what? Heights? An elevator that's afraid of heights!'

Write down the answers to the following questions.

(a) In what ways is the lift in the story the same as a present-day lift and in what ways does it differ?

(b) What would you do in the situation described in the story? Is this different from what you would do if you had the same trouble with a lift tomorrow?

(c) How long will it be before a lift that responds to spoken commands will be built?

(d) What alterations to the program would you make? (Hint — use question (a) to help you)

(e) Which modern car can you buy that talks to the driver? What other talking devices have you seen? What advantages are there for the user of a talking device?

5
Information technology

What is information technology?

Numbers, words and letters alone do not mean very much. They become information only when they are put in a sentence. For instance, the number five does not tell you anything, but if you combine with it the idea that five is the number of your house, then people will know where to find you.

The machines that can be used to store, sort, copy and transfer information belong to the world of *information technology*. This world includes pencils, typewriters, photocopiers and telephones as well as computers.

A case study: the estate agent

The offices of firms, both large and small, contain information technology. The staff of these offices all use information technology to do their jobs in a more effective way. Cathy, who works in the office of a small estate agent shown in Fig. 5.1, talks about her typical day.

'I get to work at eight thirty, open up the shop and turn on the lights and the computer. Then I open the post and sort it out so that the letters go to the right people. That's not too difficult as there are only three people working in the office, besides the two secretaries. The firm used to have two other girls working here, but the computer has speeded up the work and so there was no

Fig. 5.1 *The inside of a small estate agent's office*

Fig. 5.2 *Cathy*

Fig. 5.3 *Mrs Holmes*

need to replace them when they left.

I use the computer for two things, and my boss uses it to do other things. I type all my letters on the wordprocessor, and I also put in details of the houses that are for sale. When people come in to ask for particulars, I can easily print them out. If they don't know quite what they want I can use the computer to give them a choice. We also have the particulars of people on our mailing list so that if new houses which may interest them come on the market, the computer automatically sends them the details; it even prints the envelopes. What it doesn't do is talk to the people who come in during the day and ask them what they want. That's the most interesting side of the job. You get some interesting people in here, and a few odd ones too.'

Cathy relies a great deal on the help given by the computer. How would she cope if the power failed? She says that her boss, Mrs. Holmes, uses the machine for other things as well. Here is what she has to say.

'Cathy has already told you how we use the machine to speed up the movement of information about houses. I use the computer for another important function too – I use it to run the financial side of the business. This includes working out the bills which we have to send out and the staff wages. I'm sure you will find similar uses of computers wherever you find them in business. I've just bought a new software package that is starting to help me plan the way I spend the money for next year. This is a spreadsheet program. I have great hopes that this will show me where I need to spend more money and where I'm spending too much.'

A *spreadsheet* program uses the computer's ability to work out sums quickly. The managers of firms can now decide what is the best thing to do after having tried several different ways on a computer spreadsheet. Before computers were available, it would have taken far too long to do these calculations by hand.

ACTIVITIES

A1 Sheet
The program called **Sheet** that comes with this book is a very simple spreadsheet demonstration.

The screen in Fig. 5.4 shows the amount of money spent on wages, advertisements, materials and taxes. It also shows how much money comes into the firm. The balance is the difference between this money coming in and all the payments. The balance from one quarter of a year gets taken forward to the next quarter. The program allows the amount for each item to be changed and then calculates the changes on all the other items. It shows the pattern of change for each item using graphs.

Run the program and see the effect of altering the amount spent and the amount earned at different times.

A2 Using a data base
The program called Agent is a simple version of an estate agent's program. The

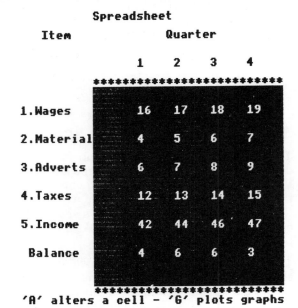

Fig. 5.4 A screen dump from the program 'Sheet'

area covered by the estate agent is a fictional town called Smallville. A map of the town is shown in Fig. 5.5.

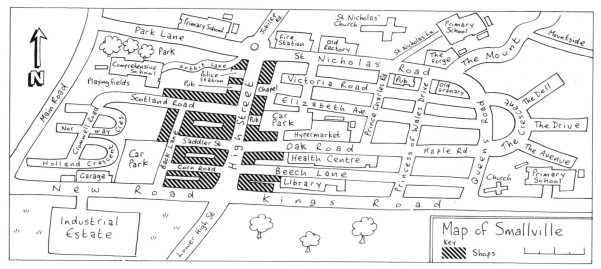

Fig. 5.5 A map of Smallville

The program allows you to find a particular house, (if you know the address), and to find houses in a specific price range or area, and of a particular size or type. When you run the program you will be asked to enter which of these ways you want to use in order to find a house. This is done using a menu. You will see the following display on the screen:

```
****************************************
              ESTATE AGENT
****************************************
Number in list at present - 50
         1. Find by price range
         2. Find by post code
         3. Find by size
         4. Find by address
         5. Find by type
         6. End search
         7. Display list

      Which do you want (1-7)?
```

Fig. 5.6 A screen dump from the 'Agent' program

If you select numbers 2, 3, 4 or 5 you will be asked to put in one more piece of information (size, area, type or address). If you try number 1, you have to put in the lowest price which you want to pay,

followed by the highest price. Once you have put in the information, the screen shows you how many of the houses on the list fit your description. For instance, a customer may walk into the estate agent's office and ask to see all the houses in a certain area. She or he may wish to live there rather than anywhere else because of the view. In the demonstration program the area around the park could be one such pleasant area. The postal code of the area around the park is SM1. Cathy would supply the customer with the required information by selecting number 2 and by entering 'SM1' when prompted for the post code. All the houses that are for sale around the park would then be listed on the screen. It is possible to select from this new smaller list using another requirement. In this way a customer can gradually narrow down the houses until he or she finds a small number to go to see.

This type of program is easy to use but it limits the user to certain tasks. A more general type of program using more complicated commands may be more powerful, but it would be more difficult to use.

It would be quite easy for your teachers to alter this program so that it uses information from your area.

Fig. 5.7 A typical wordprocessor station

Wordprocessing

Fig. 5.7 shows a wordprocessor which is a widely used piece of computing equipment. The term describes the hardware as well as the dedicated task which it does. A wordprocessing package usually consists of a keyboard, a screen, a storage device (such as a disc), a printer and the computer itself (which will contain the wordprocessing programs).

As text is typed into the computer, it appears on the screen and can be corrected before the final copy is printed, or saved permanently on the storage system. More powerful programs allow complicated functions, such as moving letters, words or blocks of text around to alter the layout. This means that altering the letter does not involve retyping it. The appropriate piece can be changed and the new version printed out with or without altering the stored

version. Several copies of the same letter can then be sent out with a different name on each one. Every letter is personal, but no retyping is necessary. Other facilities available on the program may be altering line length, putting in headings or aligning margins etc.

The introduction of a wordprocessor makes a big difference to a typist's job. It has been suggested that up to 30% of a typist's time could be saved by a wordprocessor. In other words, two typists using a wordprocessor could do as much work as three typists working without one. The work style of the typist also changes, retraining is necessary and the typist must develop new skills to adapt to the new way of working. There is certainly more strain involved in watching a VDU screen all day than in using a typewriter.

Telecommunications

The uses of information technology described so far in this chapter work in 'stand-alone mode'. That is, they can be used by a single person sitting at the keyboard using the information which is at hand. In the case of large companies this is not always the case. For instance, a chain store may be managed by its Head Office in a city many miles away. The manager will need information which is at the store to be able to decide what to do. Even data base packages, wordprocessors and spreadsheet programs work only if the information is to hand.

This problem can be overcome by linking the computer at Head Office directly to the store computer. Information can then pass quickly and directly between the computers. The telephone system is used to transfer signals between computers, just as people communicate using the telephone.

The hardware

In order to make computer signals compatible with the telephone network a device called a *modem* is used (Fig. 5.8). The modem produces a note that can be altered in pitch in sympathy with the computer signals i.e. the note is said to be *modulated* by the data. At the other end of the line another modem is used to reverse the effect, so it converts the changing note back into pulses. This is called *demodulation* (hence the word modem from the words MOdulation and DEModulation). A block diagram describing this process is shown in Fig. 5.9.

The software

Unfortunately the hardware on its own is not enough. Before the computer signals can be sent to or received from the modem, the computer has to organise these signals. The program which does the organising has to be loaded into the computer either from a special memory microchip called a 'Read Only Memory,' *ROM*, tape or disc. The program sets up the transmitter and receiver. Once the data has been exchanged

Fig. 5.8 Information can be sent by telephone line when this modem is connected to a computer

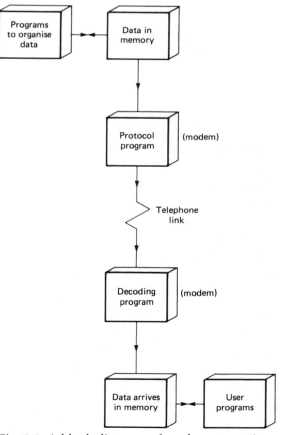

Fig. 5.9 A block diagram of modem operation

more programs will be needed to work with the data.

It is not possible for computers using different ways of organising data and different modems to send data to each other. It is now possible, however, to link up the sort of computers used in schools with computers in other organisations with the telephone network. There are several suppliers of equipment that allow customers access to their computers, Maplin Electronic Supplies and Display Electronics are two examples. Micronet 800 is an organisation that sells computer software over the telephone to enthusiasts. This organisation is the first of what will be many paperless publishing companies. Fig. 5.10 shows how it is arranged.

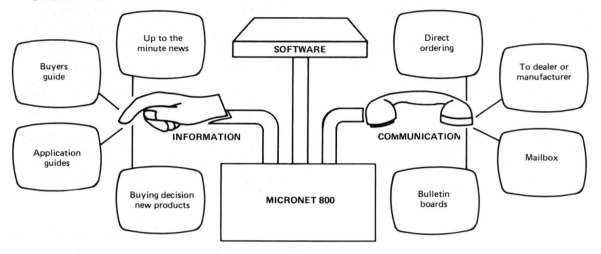

Fig. 5.10 *The organisation of an electronic publishing company*

Electronic mail

Electronic mail is more than just linking two remote computers together. A basic system using just two machines is possible but limited. The two operators would need to agree when they are to link up, and it would not be possible to leave messages on such a system. Electronic mail systems use a central coordinating computer. Remote computers link into this machine and messages are passed through it to other subscribers.

Schools in several counties in England use this form of communication to exchange games fixtures. Arranging next Saturday's football matches with neighbouring schools by phone is a difficult and frustrating business for games staff. Many phone calls and verbal messages are needed just to arrange when they are available to talk to each other. Using an electronic mail system, messages can be typed into the central computer and relayed to the other school when it links up to the network.

The British Telecom network

British Telecom has set up its own data network called Prestel. This can work as an electronic mail system as well as an information system. Subscribers have their own number which allows other users to contact. They also each have a code number which only they know. This code number has to be entered when they first connect to the system. The account which matches the code number is charged according to how much use is made of the system. Prestel makes a great deal of information easy to get at. Examples of this are train and plane timetables, financial information and, entertainment guides. Since the system is two-way (*interactive*) it is possible to book seats on planes and to order theatre tickets. Moving money between accounts in building societies and banks is now possible too. If you have over a certain amount of money in one building society you get this sort of service free.

Other firms make use of Prestel to advertise their services but the easy access is not suited to all firms. For example, Thomas Cook, the travel firm, has a system using the same technology as Prestel but which allows access to it only if you are one of their agents or have an agreement with them. This 'Holiday-Maker' network is fully interactive too and it is possible to book holidays through it. The system is being improved all the time and it will be possible for agents to use the computer power of the company's central computers via intelligent terminals that can cope with questions put to them in English. Go and have a look at the travel agents near your school and you will see information technology at work.

Ceefax and Oracle

These two teletex services are supplied by the BBC and ITV. They both work on the same system and the hardware that is needed works for both. What is needed is simply an adapted television set.

The various pages of information sent out by these *viewdata systems* are transmitted in turn, a few at a time, like the slides in a carousel projector. The system is not highly interactive. The viewer can select which page to view. On some pages however there are 'hidden' items which can be seen by pressing the reveal button on the control panel. A recent addition to this form of data transmission is computer programs. The BBC have started to transmit programs on certain pages of Ceefax. A separate adapter is needed for the BBC microcomputer in order to 'down load' this software and run it. Other countries have their own versions of teletex — *Telidon* in Canada, *Captain* in Japan and *Antiope* in France. The cost of television sets with built-in decoders for this type of data transmission is falling. It is therefore likely that many more homes will be using this system in the near future.

ACTIVITIES

A1 Visit your local town centre and survey the shops that are using information technology. What are they using it for? How has it changed their business? Has it made the store a different place to work in?

A2 Cut out from newspapers the advertisements for office computers and make a poster showing the many types of machine there are. Should you include photocopiers as well as computer equipment?

A3 Using the estate agent program accompanying this book, suggest suitable houses for the following people:
(a) A young married couple, buying their first home who have about £20,000 to spend.
(b) A single girl who has about £19,000 to spend and who wants a small terraced house.
(c) A company manager who wants a large secluded house and can pay up to £65,000.
(d) A retired couple who want a smaller house than their present three bedroomed house. They can pay as much as it takes.

TOPICS FOR DISCUSSION

D1 The estate agent program has several parts left out. What other things should the user be able to do with the program?

D2 What sort of training is involved when new technology is first introduced? Why do school leavers not have the skills needed by business? Should they be taught them in schools?

D3 How does the introduction of new technology change the number of jobs in an office?

EXERCISES

1 Copy and complete the following sentences.

(a) Information can be made up from ....

(b) Machines that belong to the world of office technology can ...., ..., ..., ... and .... information.

(c) Three examples of information technology machines are ....

(d) Three examples of places to find information technology are: ....

(e) The number of people working in the estate agent's office .... when the computer was introduced.

(f) The person who benefitted most from the computer in the estate agent's office was ....

(g) A computer that moves text around is called ....

(h) The data base on the estate agent's computer contained the address, ..., ..., ... and the price of each house.

(i) A software package that sets out numbers in columns and recalculates these numbers if one is changed is called a ....

(j) .... is needed to run a firm effectively. In order to collect it, a manager may travel to different .... of the firm but she or he is more likely to use a data ....

(k) 'Stand alone' is the computer jargon for a computer which is not ....

(l) Getting computers linked together requires both the .... and the .... to be matched up.

(m) ...., ... and .... are three examples of firms offering electronic customer services.

(n) Prestel offers both an .... system and an .... system.

(o) The two viewdata services offered by BBC and ITV are .... and respectively.

2 Write a paragraph on each of the following themes.

(a) Being able to use information technology is a vital skill for all school pupils today.

(b) The type of data base that I would like to access.

(c) The dangers of information technology.

Write in sentences and explain any claims you make.

6
Simulation and learning with computers

What are models and simulations?

Fig. 6.1 shows some things that seem to have little in common. What has a puppet in common with a model aeroplane? What is the link between the baby doll and the steam engine? The answer is that they all behave like the real things which they model. The puppet moves like a human being: the plane flies in the same way as a real plane: the baby doll makes noises and 'performs' like a real baby: the steam engine works like a full sized engine. They are all models of a real object. They are called *simulations*. We can use them to discover how the original behaves and so we can learn how to control it.

Models do not have to look or behave exactly like the object which they model. The puppet does not talk, but it is still an entertaining lifelike object. Roy Hudd's Emu makes its feelings known, but unlike the real bird it does not lay eggs! Models can be useful even if they do not model every part of the original.

The choice of model depends on what you want to model. The more lifelike the simulation, the more it costs. Microcomputers now make it possible to make simulations that are very lifelike at very low cost. They can be programmed with the same rules that make the original system work. The output from the computer can be a list of numbers showing how the model

Fig. 6.1 A puppet, a model aeroplane, a baby doll and a steam engine. These are examples of models and simulations

behaves or, better still, a moving picture. The computer simulation can run at any speed. If the real situation is too slow the computer program can be speeded up to make the model much faster. Patterns may be easier to see that way.

Computer simulations can be used to find out about the things which they model or to teach people how to operate them. They give students the chance to try things that would be too expensive or too dangerous to try in real life. They are therefore being used more and more in schools and industry to help to train and to educate people.

Simulations in industrial training

Some of the skills needed in work are difficult to learn in a short time. Experience is needed. A way of giving wide experience in a short time is through the use of computer simulations which can be cheaper than training using the real equipment. Computer-driven simulations also allow the teacher to set up situations which might be dangerous in real life and so teach the best way of dealing with them.

Simulations are being used to train many people, from nuclear-reactor operators to pilots, from tank-drivers to machine-tool operators. The activity program with this chapter is the sort of simulation that might be found in an industrial setting. It allows you to try your hand at running a nuclear reactor.

The flight simulator
A most exciting use of simulation is in the training of pilots. The flight simulator (Fig. 6.2) is a total simulation of the conditions in a plane before, during and after flight.

The flight simulator is the ultimate in simulations and modelling. It makes it possible to train pilots to fly commercial aircraft without them ever leaving the ground. They can be tested in situations that may arise in flight, but which would be too dangerous to try during a normal flight. The running costs of the simulation are much lower than those of the real aircraft. The simulation can be frozen at any instant and situations discussed before the pilot has to handle them or after they have just taken place. The same situation can be practised

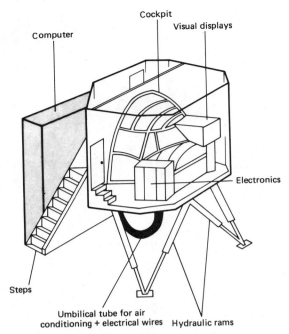

Fig. 6.2 The structure of a flight simulator

until the pilot's reactions are right.

The pilots of real aircraft use several senses to make the plane behave in a controlled way. They use eyes to scan the instruments which record the movement of the plane and to view the scene outside during landing and take-off. The sense of touch plays an important part in the feel of the aircraft – how it responds to the pushing and pulling of the controls. The flight simulator is an expensive and lifelike simulation because it can fool all the pilot's senses. The pilot cannot tell the difference between the simulator and the plane it simulates. To make all the right noises, movement and views of the outside in the correct way needs not one but several computers.

The simulator itself is a room the size of a small mobile classroom mounted on hydraulic rams (Fig. 6.3). Outside the simulator are the computers used to control the machine. The rams shown in Fig. 6.4 are controlled by one of the computers and they move the box around so that the senses of all those sitting inside the box are fooled into thinking that the box is flying.

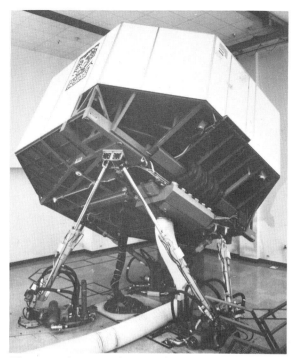

Fig. 6.3 The outside of a flight simulator. The cabin can move from almost ground level to a height of 4 or 5 metres

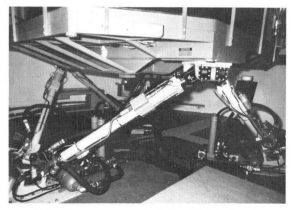

Fig. 6.4 The movement of the flight simulator cabin is caused by these hydraulic rams. They are similar to those on a road digger

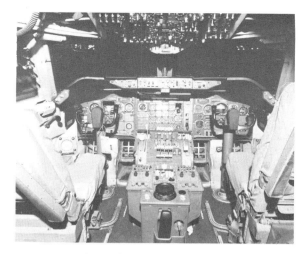

Fig. 6.5 (a) The interior of a real Boeing 747. (b) The interior of a 747 flight simulator. All the dials and controls are linked and work as they do in the real plane.

Inside the box is a mock-up of the plane cockpit shown in Fig. 6.5. All the instruments are worked by computer. The control sticks and levers can be moved by the pilot and the correct feel of each one is generated by the computer. Outside the windows are mounted

video monitors. These are fed with computer-generated views of the outside. There has been a lot of progress in recent years and the visual computer can now make up a daylight view in 3-D of a selected airport (Fig. 6.6). The view will change as the plane flies

Fig. 6.6 This daylight scene of an airport, as seen from an aircraft on final approach, is drawn by computer

around the simulation; the night-time view of airports can be generated as well (Fig. 6.7). At the rear of the simulator platform sits the instructor (Fig. 6.8). He has a control console that allows him to select all types of situations for the trainee pilot to cope with. For example, the weather outside the plane can be simulated; storms can be generated where the movement of the simulator will be violent, just like the real plane. The way the pilot deals with these is watched, and any mistakes he makes can be corrected.

The programming of a simulator starts with a basic understanding of where the pilot belongs in the whole system. He is fed with information about the aircraft through his senses. He then alters the aircraft and senses the alterations. This system has to be changed into a set of rules for the computer to work out what to do with the hydraulic

rams, the monitors and all the instruments.

While the programming is taking place, the machinery itself is being put together. The construction of the mock-up is not that different from a real aircraft and where possible the simulator will use the same instruments and controls as the real plane. Finally, the whole simulator is tested, a few parts at a time, to check that it all functions. The ultimate test is then for a qualified pilot to 'take it up and throw it around the sky'.

Some of the thrill of being in a simulator can be found using programs that have been written for school micros, such shown as in Fig. 6.9, but the visual image on its own lacks the mixture of fairground thrills and realism that the flight simulator captures. School micros cannot include motion, feel and sound as well as the visual image – yet!

Fig. 6.7 A night-time view of the area around an airport. The lights are drawn on TV screens by computer

Fig. 6.8 This view of a 747 simulator shows the seat for the instructor on the left-hand side. From the consol on the left any emergency can be simulated

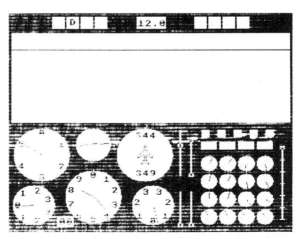

Fig. 6.9 A screen dump from 'DACC 747 simulator'

Computers in schools

In this section a number of uses of computers in the classroom will be described.

The first school lessons in which the computer appeared were mathematics classes. The computer was used to teach maths and computer studies. Computer studies is now one of the subjects taught in almost all secondary schools. It has been taught for many years and the sort of computers which it investigates and the information it deals with are not modern. In computer studies teachers try to explain the mathematics and logic behind the operation of computers. The skills involved in programming are practised and knowledge of the ways in which firms use main-frame computers is also taught. Usually a maths teacher organises the subject. The sort of computing dealt with often avoids the use of computers in control and communication, it is usually data processing which is taught. There are some employers who do not think that computer studies is a worthwhile subject to take because the computing it teaches is so limited.

As the size and cost of computers have fallen so teachers have found it possible to buy more machines or to move them around. Other subjects are now able to make use of them.

Simulation in school

Teachers in a growing number of areas other than computer studies are using micro-computer simulations to help to teach skills and to help pupils think.

One well-known simulation is the exploration of the Mary Rose (a Tudor warship which sank off the Isle of Wight in 1545). Fig. 6.10 shows a 'screen dump' from the program. In this set of programs the pupil can steer a boat around the Solent and detect various objects on the sea bed. The simulation teaches bearings, diving techniques and the history of Tudor warships. It is a good simulation since the pupil is in control – the program does not drive the pupil, it allows exploration. It is simulating a situation that could not be experienced in the classroom.

Fig. 6.10 A screen dump from 'The Mary Rose' program

Using a computer simulation is not always an advantage. Computer simulations are sometimes used when there is no need for a simulation at all. For example, one simulation in chemistry teaching sets up a computer to behave like a simple chemical test. One chemical is run out of a measuring tube into another chemical which changes colour at the right concentration. In this example the chemicals and equipment cost far less than the microcomputer. There is no reason for the simulation – the real experiment should have been done instead. However, the computer is the only way to do some experiments in the classroom. Programs can be bought that allow physics students to study the paths of planets around the Sun, to alter the distances between the planets themselves and the sun, and to change the planet sizes. There is no way to do this sort of experimentation other than by using a computer simulation.

Computers in science teaching

Another use of computer power is to monitor experiments. Fig. 6.11 shows a microcomputer set up with an interface box. The box is connected to a coil that supports the ballbearing at the top and a trap-door sensor that converts the passage of the ballbearing into an electrical signal. The computer can then control the dropping of the ball, time its flight and work out the value of its acceleration due to the force of gravity.

Fig. 6.11 *This photograph shows a BBC microcomputer linked to equipment to measure how much a ball bearing speeds up when it is dropped. The computer controls the experiment and automatically calculates the results*

Computers in teaching humanities

Other subjects are exploring the use of computers in teaching. Subjects like history and geography have started to make use of programs which allow pupils to select information from data bases and to use the results to test out ideas. 'Quest' is one such package. See Fig. 6.12. This set of programs has been used to record census information. The data is made up of records of information about people who used to live in a particular town or area. Each record has fields showing the name, date of birth, occupation and address of the individual. History teachers and their students can make use of this information in the same way as historians who spend all of their time looking for patterns in census returns. The computer brings the benefit of speed and accuracy to such searches. For example, it is possible to easily find out how many people were unemployed or worked at a particular trade. If these figures were compared with a recent census then the way in which employment has changed could be mapped out. Using several census returns it is possible to investigate infant mortality and the movement of families around the country.

Fig. 6.12

Computers in language teaching

Language teachers are using computers to help to teach vocabulary. The pupil is given words and then tested on them and a running score is kept. This type of training is different from the other forms described here because the computer, rather than the pupil, is in control and decides how the lesson goes. Since they rely on a lot of text these programs are limited by the size of computer memory. Until the price of large memory comes down it does not seem likely that computers will be used widely in the teaching languages.

This section has shown several different uses of computers in the classroom. The computer can be used as:

1 a data logger for experiments;
2 a tool for investigating census returns and other data bases;
3 a modelling tool to allow pupils to try different ways of doing things;
4 a simulator to allow pupils to explore new situation;
5 a training/testing machine that programs the pupil.

TOPICS FOR DISCUSSION

D1 Will advanced computers replace teachers?

D2 Instead of coming to school would you rather stay at home in front of a computer screen? Are there good reasons for learning in a group of people of your own age?

D3 Using a computer to help with, say, science is not always a good thing. Doing the calculations for an experiment helps

you to practise mathematics at the same time as seeing the science. Is this a good reason against the use of computers in school science see Fig. 6.13?

D4 Computer models and simulations can be wrong because the program takes the theory too far. Is there therefore a danger that pupils will be taught incorrectly by computers?

D5 Which is it better to buy — a set of text books or a computer?

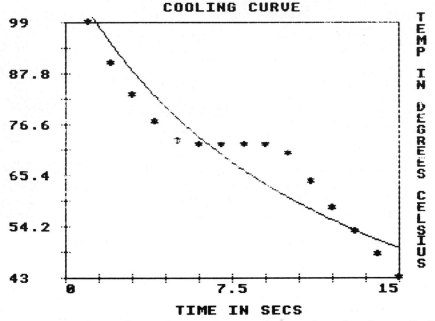

Fig. 6.13 This graph was drawn by a microcomputer using results taken by pupils in a science lesson. The pupils did not have to decide on the scale or plot the points themselves. It was a lot easier for them than doing it by hand

ACTIVITY

Electricity in Britain is made at power stations that are fired by fossil fuels, like oil and coal, or heated by nuclear reaction, (Fig. 6.14). The people who run these nuclear power stations are highly trained. They have spent years learning the basic skills of engineering and they are then taught how to manage the reactor. One of the programs supplied with this book,

Reactor, is a simulation of a nuclear reactor. The way it behaves is similar to a **Magnox** nuclear reactor and it is possible, through using the program, to learn the basic ideas and problems of nuclear power generation. In order to have some idea of how to control the program, you should read following explanation.

Power stations make electricity by changing water into steam using heat. The

Fig. 6.14 Oldbury 'Magnox' Nuclear Power Station near Thornbury, Avon

steam then drives the electricity generators. Fig. 6.15 is a diagram of a nuclear reactor. In a reactor the heat comes from breaking up fuel rather than from burning it. Some materials, like uranium, are **radioactive** and will break up very easily. Inside the reactor are cans of uranium. As the uranium breaks up it gives off heat and small pieces of atoms known as **fission chips**. Some of these chips, the **neutrons**, will bombard other atoms and make them break up too to give off even more heat and chips. Unless the breakdown of uranium is carefully controlled, a **runaway** chain reaction starts and the reactor becomes uncontrollable. The reactor is controlled by rods which work like the damper in a fire. When they are lowered into the

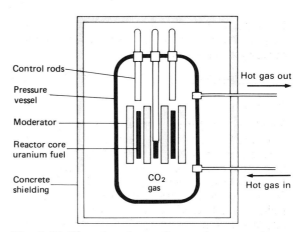

Fig. 6.15 The structure of a nuclear reactor

reactor they absorb the neutrons and the reaction slows down. As an emergency measure, boron balls can be dropped into some reactors to shut them down in an emergency. The heat from the chain reaction is taken out of the reactor by blowing gas through it. The gas is pumped around by a circulator turbine.

The operator has to work the reactor up to a critical condition. This is when the reaction is only just controlled rather than shutting down or running out of control. He does this by raising the rods and watching the neutron flux until it steadies at 32,000. He will need to set the rods at the right depth to keep the neutrons at this level. As the reaction starts up, the temperature of the reactor rises slowly. If the reactor is controlled it will stop rising at 363°C. At this stage the gas is blown in by turning on the turbine. Power is then generated from the hot gas and fed to the national grid.

Mistakes that can be made by the operators are:

1 letting the reaction build up too fast — this can result in a runaway;
2 allowing the temperature of the reactor to get too high — if this happens, the rods may stick and control will be lost;
3 allowing the radioactivity to get too high — this is dangerous for workers and usually occurs if 1 is allowed to happen.

It can be overcome by dropping emergency boron into the reactor, but this will shut it down and require a lot of expensive repair work;
4 starting the turbines too early — this will result in low temperature steam hitting the blades of the generator causing them to break up.

The simulation program uses these keys:

R — raise the control rods;

L — lower the control rods;

E — emergency rod drop (drops the rods in all the way);

B — drops boron balls into the reactor to try to shut it down;

S — increases the turbine speed;

Z — decreases the turbine speed;

T — turbine trip (stops the turbine).

The readings you should aim for are:

1 neutron flux of 32000;
2 cap (reactor top) temperature 363°C;
3 inlet (reactor bottom) temperature 347°C;
4 turbine speed 2100 rev min.

If you allow the reactor to get out of hand and fail to shut it down before the temperature and flux levels make it impossible to control you will reach the **China syndrome**. At this stage the reactor will melt down into one mass of radioactive, hot and poisonous metal and melt down through the ground until it meets water. At this stage an explosion will occur which will destroy the site and spread lethal doses of radiation over a wide area. Take care, but remember that its only a **simulation**!

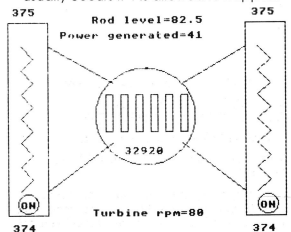

Fig. 6.16 *A screen dump from the program 'Reactor'*

The school of the future?

The following story is set a few years in the future. Read it and answer the questions before you consider the topics for discussion.

John was feeling miserable. He turned over and hit the alarm clock so hard that it bounced off the bedside table and rolled on the floor. It didn't stop ringing.

It was a school day. He knew that there was no way, short of blowing all the fuses in the house, that he could avoid those four boring hours in front of the VDU. It wouldn't be so bad if he was allowed to set up two-way links with his friends while he interacted. As it was, the School Network would not allow this for another week.

TOO MUCH UNNECESSARY
COMMUNICATION WITH PEERS

It had blinked at him last week.

TWO-WAY LINKS BLOCKED FOR TWO
WEEKS

Surely things were easier in his Mum's day. All the teachers did then was move you for part of a lesson, at the very most you got sent out. You weren't cut off for two weeks.

John dressed and ate breakfast. At nine o'clock sharp the bell on the VDU sounded. The system would send a warning to his

Mum at work if he refused its summons. Mum would then come panting up from the other VDU in the cellar and give him a good going over. He had to log on. What a bore.

The first module was a simple French lesson. The screen showed him films of parts of France, French people talking to each other, French vineyards, French trains. Every now and then, just when he was dozing off, the screen would freeze and, in that grim artificial female voice the teaching network always used, he would be prompted for a reply in French. If he got it wrong the system tried in its infant way to try to find out why he found that part difficult. John had long since given up trying to goad it. Answering it in silly ways didn't annoy it — making it think he was an idiot didn't convince it. All the time it kept its temper and showed little emotion in its synthetic voice.

Time for a break. The oven in the kitchen yelled that it was ready and John, having finished module one, left the screen and collected his mid-morning snack. The plastic cup of soup and the bread roll went down well. The House even allowed him to put on the radio. He listened to the local DJ for a while. It wasn't loud enough though. The neighbours had complained again to the Computer Centre and the House would not allow him to turn it up any further.

Back to work. Adventure game. This was a little better. The history topic he was following covered the Egyptians. He had written a folder on the Pharaohs and had cut out illustrations from the Sunday papers. He was taken with the attempts they had made at brain surgery. Even using primitive tools they had opened up skulls and drilled holes in the bone to relieve pressure. This adventure game was based on Egyptian surgery. John needed to show skill in deciding who to operate on. He had a choice of King, slave or trader. Over the years the correct choice and the speed of operation decided the growth of the town. He enjoyed the game. It meant something to him because it was part of the subject he was studying. He could imagine the doctors in their robes deciding who would be the best patient. So many of the tasks the Network set were just programs on their own and meant little. A bit like seeing a TV programme without being introduced to the topic first and not talking it

over after. This game fitted in with what he knew.

Lunch time and half way through the session. John had to get outside. The VDU was beginning to give him a headache. It got some people that way. Some of his friends had reached the point when they could only watch it for a few minutes at a time. The doctor said it was tension due to the forthcoming end-of-year exams and that there was nothing wrong with their eyes or the VDU. John thought otherwise. Perhaps he should complain of a headache and the network would shut down for a week — no chance!

The afternoon session was a killer. Two hours of unbroken maths. Train and test; train and test. His head began to whirl. He lost all track of time and it was only when the end-of-session bell sounded in the middle of a sticky matrix multiplication that he realised the time. The network graded him on the day and updated his mark file. He was averaging between grade 4 and 3 at the moment. Not bad. Hard copy of his homework spilled out of the matrix printer and the network signed off with its usual

'HAVE A NICE DAY — BYE'.

Why did they allow those American phrases to creep into the software?

John slumped in the chair exhausted. Eventually he commanded the House to connect to Shane, his best friend. Shane had finished school work some time ago and was ready for some fun.
'Tell you what John, how about some vintage stuff?'
John couldn't wait: 'What do you mean Shane?'
'There's a great oldie on the box tonight — ET — how about coming round and watching it together?'
John sighed — 'Not more TV, I can't stand it. I've been stuck in front of that thing for four hours and all you can come up with is another two hours of flicker — no thanks. I'm going to do something far more interesting. Something where I can decide the speed. Something where I make up the images. You know what you can do with your film! I'm going to read a book.'
John logged off and joined the human race.

EXERCISES

1 Read the short story about the School of the Future and answer the following questions.

(a) Why is John's house called The House. What can it do that your house cannot?

(b) Why was John banned from setting up electronic links with his friends?

(c) What was the job the Network had to do with John?

(d) What sort of job did John's Mum have?

(e) What was the main difference between his mother's job and the job that most mums do today?

(f) What had John done to try to goad the Network?

(g) Why had he not managed to annoy the Network?

(h) How would the Network have tried to find out what he found difficult? How do teachers do this with you?

(i) How could the oven yell?

(j) The House would not allow him to turn the radio up. What must the neighbours have done to get this block placed on the House computer?

(k) Why did John find the adventure game more interesting than the other two lessons in the day?

(l) Which subject made him lose track of time? Explain why it was this one?

(m) John had the chance to go to his friend's house to watch a film. Why did he not go?

(n) John opted to read a book rather than watch a film. What reasons did he give for reading a book?

The following questions are more general.

2 What is a simulation?

3 Give three reasons for using simulations to train people?

4 Listed below are some reasons why schools may not be able to use computers in every subject. Try to place them in order – the one that may be most true the first and the one that may be least true the last:

(a) microcomputers are expensive;

(b) software is expensive;

(c) not all subjects can benefit from computer software;

(d) teachers do not know how to use computers and are frightened of them;

(e) students do not know how to use computers and do not want to learn;

(f) the right software has not been written;

(g) parents do not want their children to use computers;

(h) computers are too fragile and students will break them;

(i) computers can only be used by experts.

TOPICS FOR DISCUSSION

D1 Flight simulators are used to train pilots to fly planes they have never flown before. Describe how you would feel the next time you fly on holiday if the captain announced that he had never before flown the plane you were in but that he had been converted on a simulator.

D2 Here is the answer to a question: 'Simulators have a serious drawback. They can be programmed to behave like the real thing but their programs do not include situations that could not be predicted.'
What was the question?

D3 What reasons would you give if, some years in the future, you had to persuade someone not to close your school and replace it with VDUs in all the student's homes?

7
Research and development

Modern design

There are five stages in the design of modern goods. These five stages and the way that computers are used in them will now be described.

Stage one: feasibility

Before anyone will pay money for something to be built they have to be convinced that it is possible to build a product that will do the job. If the job is the relay of telephone calls across the Atlantic then feasibility means proving that a satellite can be built, launched into orbit, adjusted and that it will work. There is no second try with a satellite. Things have to work the first time. Even the space shuttle cannot recover satellites from altitudes as high as 22000 km such as those used for transmitting telephone conversations, data and video signals.

The length of time taken to prove that the idea is possible will depend on many things. It can take between six months and a year to prove that a satellite system will work if it is built. This period of investigation is described as a *feasibility stage*. Computers are involved at this stage in several ways. Firstly, they are used to model the satellite. They will be programmed to behave as a

Fig. 7.1 The artist of the future?

satellite does when it is launched. This model is not made out of plastic or wood or any solid material; it is a series of programs held in the computer. The output from these programs may be a series of numbers that the scientists and engineers can understand.

Secondly, towards the end of the feasibility stage, the output may be converted into pictures or line film. There may even be a visual computer simulation of the satellite as it would appear to someone near to it in space. This simulation would be like Fig. 7.2. It can be understood by people other than

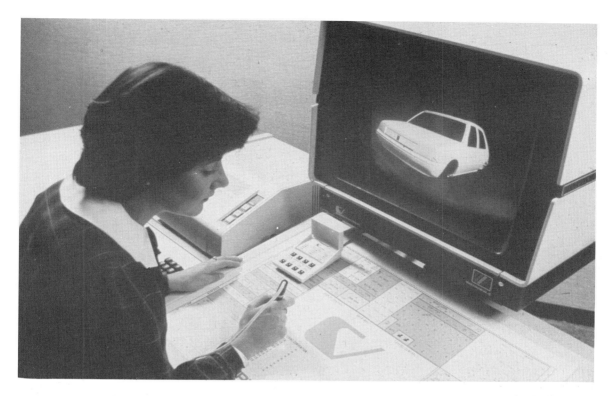

Fig. 7.2 Computer models of systems can look like the car on the screen here. This shows the buyer exactly how the car will appear when it is built

scientists, and it may be used to convince the person putting up the money that the project is possible. Thirdly, computers will be used to work out the cost of building the system. This use of computers is called *financial modelling.*

Stage two: project definition

The next stage is to identify the problems and to work out how to solve them. This is called *project definition.*

Consider the satellite system. Once the contract for the system has been won then the satellite design has to be broken down into small parts. Each part may be separately modelled on a computer. These parts will have to work together to make the whole system do what it is supposed to. This can only be guaranteed if the way in which

each part behaves is known. The computer will be used at the project definition stage to give this information.

The type of computer used at this stage is different from any that you will see in school. The models which are programmed into it need to work in *real-time* (they must operate at the speed at which the real thing works). There are many numbers that must be taken into account when programming this sort of model, and digital computers are not the fastest way of accounting for large numbers of large numbers. Instead a different type of computer called an *analogue* computer, shown in Fig. 7.3, is used. This computer is not built out of logic chips but a series of amplifiers instead. These amplifiers are not unlike those in your cassette player or radio. The satellite system is modelled on these amplifiers by changing the volume settings and the tone controls. (Fig. 7.4) A model may involve scores of amplifiers. Sometimes a separate digital computer is used to set up all the analogue computer controls and to print out the results. These computers can be made to run at any time scale. If the model is

Fig. 7.3 *The control panel of the analogue computer. The control knobs can be seen on each side. The wires in the middle are there to wire up the various amplifiers*

a very fast one, like a collision, then it may be useful to run the model at a slower speed than real time. If, on the other hand, the model is slow moving, like a space probe, then it may be better to speed up the action.

Up to 18 months may have been spent on this stage of the project. At the end of the feasibility stage the company will know how each part of the system should behave. It will have a much better idea of the cost of the project and it will also have a working model of the system in its computers. When the first part of the system is built this model will be used to compare the part with its model.

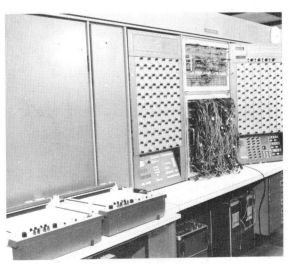

Fig. 7.4 *Models of satellites and missiles can be programmed into this analogue computer*

Fig. 7.5 A satellite or missile is mounted on the motion table and readings are taken to ensure that it will work properly. The 'egg boxes' around the table are there to absorb radiowaves that bounce off the walls and cause interference

Stage three: development

It is only at this stage that parts of the satellite system will be built. Until this time all that has happened is the testing of ideas and theories using computer models. Now those models will be built and tested to see how they behave compared with computer predictions.

The equipment needed to test a complete satellite is made up of a *flight table*, sensors and a computer. The flight table, shown in Fig. 7.5, is a mounting for the satellite which can move it in three directions at once — left/right, up/down and rotate. The mounting is driven by hydraulic pressure rams (as in the pilot's flight simulator) controlled by computer. The satellite is bolted onto the

table, and sensors are mounted on and around it to measure the behaviour of the satellite. Computer programs are then run with the satellite turned on. The table will be moved around to make the satellite move as it would in space under various conditions, and measurements from the sensors are then compared with those predicted by the computer model. If there are differences these must be explained otherwise there may be problems when the satellite is launched. It may be that the computer model has overlooked some basic effects. If so, then the computer model has to be altered. On the other hand, the satellite hardware may not have been built exactly as it should have been. This too must be corrected.

Each part of a satellite has to stand up to

Fig. 7.6 *The item to be tested is placed in the centrifuge on the right. The lid can be shut so experiments are done in a vacuum. Notice the use of a microcomputer to control and analyse the results of experiments*

Fig. 7.7 *The finished product*

Stage four: evaluation

The evaluation stage gives the people designing the satellite time to take stock of what has been built. They will alter the models to make them fit the results of tests as closely as possible, and they may alter the design to make the system perform better. At the end of this stage, which may last as long as two years, they will have a complete idea of how the final product will behave. They may have parts of a satellite or even a whole satellite built. They know that it will work.

Stage five: production

The models that have been proved have now to be built. This will mean drawing, making and putting together all the parts that the models have shown are needed.

It would be wrong to say that drawing out the design is done only at this stage. From stage three onwards, drawings will have been made, and altered as the design changed. At stage five the final design will be drawn. In large companies, the draughtspersons now use specialist computers to aid their design and drawing.

Once the drawings have been put on the computer by the draughtsperson there are several benefits. The computer system can check the drawing for simple mistakes. In a complicated wiring diagram it will look for wires that lead nowhere. In a drawing of a mechanical part it will check that the parts fit together with the correct amount of space

rough treatment when it is launched; it will spend its life in the vacuum of space; its temperature will change over a much greater range than that found naturally on the Earth and the side facing the Sun will be cooked whilst the side in shadow will fall hundreds of degrees below freezing. The satellite hardware has to be shown to work and to continue to work in the conditions found in orbit. This development work is called *environmental testing*.

The large forces that occur when a rocket is launched are simulated using a giant roundabout. The satellite is mounted on the arm of the centrifuge and sensors are attached to it (see Fig. 7.6). The arm is then driven round and the satellite is exposed to simulated take-off forces. A similar test will be carried out in a large vacuum chamber. Giant ovens may be used to simulate the cooking due to the Sun's rays in space.

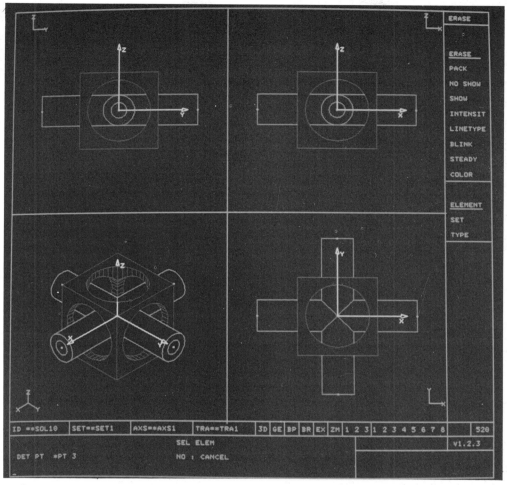

Fig. 7.8 *The screen display of a computer-aided design (CAD) station*

between them (Fig. 7.8). The same computer can produce a detailed list of parts. It can work out the cost of the design, and if the design is to be made out of metal, the computer will also produce the tape needed by the computer-controlled machines that will manufacture the part. This not only saves time (and jobs) but it stops mistakes happening when the drawing is read by a manual machine operator.

During the production stage the design has to be altered slightly to make the product possible to build. Sometimes there is a pre-production run just to work out the problems of manufacture. In the most advanced factories there are direct links between the computer-design system and the computer-controlled machine tools. No tapes have to be recorded. The designer is almost, but not quite, able to draw out the design, press a button and sit back while a machine in some other part of the factory makes that part exactly as it was drawn.

How is a computer-aided design terminal operated?

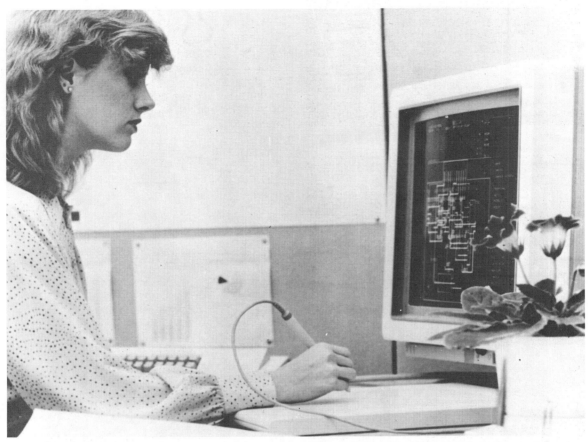

Fig. 7.9 The terminal of a computer-aided design system. The operator uses a touch pad to draw with

Fig. 7.9 shows the hardware of a computer-aided design station. The terminal is made up of a monitor, keyboard and graphics tablet. It is linked to a mini-computer which stores the software and the data base of previous drawings which act as building blocks. This hardware is expensive. A single terminal may cost tens of thousands of pounds, and much of this cost is for the screen. It is usually a colour screen, to help to pick out the different parts of the design, but it is not an ordinary colour monitor. The designs produced on it have to be very accurate, so

the picture has to be far more accurately drawn than is possible on a colour monitor.

The draughtsperson uses the keyboard, amongst other things, to send and to fetch drawings to and from the computer store, to command the computer to check the drawing and to produce a parts list. The graphics tablet is the drawing tool. On the tablet pad is a menu which can be chosen from just by pressing the pen on the menu part of the pad. A short beep tells the designer that the computer has received the instruction. The menu allows a choice of lines, cubes, squares, circles and many other shapes and the software is programmed to understand freehand symbols too. Fig. 7.10 shows the way in which one system may work. The pen

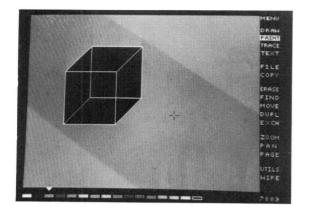

Fig. 7.10(a) The cursor is moved to the right of the screen and a variety of shapes and drawings can be selected from the system memory. In this case a cube has been picked. Moving the cursor back to the drawing area allows the user to place the cube where it is needed.

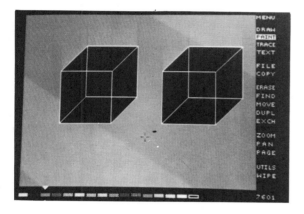

Fig. 7.10(b) The cube can then be duplicated by placing the cursor in other positions

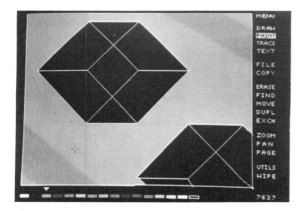

Fig. 7.10(c) Some CAD systems allow the whole screen or part of the screen to be rotated. In this case the rotation has been through 45 degrees. More sophisticated systems do the same sorts of things to 3-D drawings and allow the user to view the drawings from different angles. They also allow the eyepoint to move too so that the drawing can be viewed from any point in space both outside the shape and inside it.

is moved to the menu to select cubes. The pen is then pressed on the pad where the cubes are to be drawn and cubes then appear at these places. Making the pen draw a semicircle clockwise rotates the drawing clockwise. Other movements can duplicate parts of the drawing, change its size, rub out,

change the colour and add other drawings to parts of the new drawing.

There is a chance to experience the power of these systems in a small way by using the computer program which comes with this book. Try the following activity.

ACTIVITY

The program **Designer** is a simple computer-aided design program. It allows you to try some of the things that can be done on a full-sized design system including: drawing lines; drawing circles; drawing rectangles; drawing triangles; using a small data base of building blocks; saving drawings; loading drawings.

The position of the pen on the screen shows up as a cross. The cross is moved around using the arrow keys at the top right of the keyboard or by using a joystick. Down the right-hand side of the screen is a menu of options. To select these options position the dot over the one you want

and press

```
RETURN
```

or the FIRE button on the joystick.

To draw any of the shapes on the menu, you move the dot to the start position on the screen, press

```
RETURN
```

move to the finish position and again press

```
RETURN
```

The shape will then be drawn. Other instructions are given with the program.

Have a go at designing the following:

1 a plan of a kitchen;
2 a racing car;
3 a classroom;
4 a dress.

EXERCISES

Answer the first four questions in written sentences.

1 What are the stages which a project, like a satellite, goes through before it is built?
2 Work out how long a satellite takes to build from the idea stage to putting it into orbit, using the times given for the length of each stage.
3 Why does a project like a satellite take so long? What may happen if the time taken is shorter?
4 Why are computers used to aid design?

5 Match up the list of words with the gaps in the following sentences: monitor; graphics tablet; faster
    (a) The .... is the most expensive part of a computer-aided design terminal.
    (b) A .... is used instead of paper and pencil in modern drawing offices.
    (c) Computers do not necessarily make designing ....

6 Make up a word search using the following words: graphics; tablets; light-pen; draughtsperson; monitor; computer; terminal; design; keyboard.

TOPICS FOR DISCUSSION

D1 'Destructive testing is better done traditionally.' Why might you agree with this statement?
D2 When Computer Aided Design (CAD) aids and Computer Aided Manufacturing machines are linked together it is possible to make complex pieces very quickly. It is also possible to produce expensive mistakes very easily too. How is this possible and what steps do firms take to make it less likely?
D3 CAD terminals can be used to produce new works of art. Do you know how this can be done? Is it a good idea? Are the works of art really artistic?

8
Files on people

Files: old and new

An example of a file with you on it

You may be on a file already; your school may use a computer to help with subject choices (options). The options listed in this chapter are from a fictional school, but they are just like the options from a real school. Collecting together the options from all the students is a long and complicated task.

The subjects for Tolkien School have been arranged in groups. Students can opt for only one subject from each group. They do not have a completely free choice of subject as in some schools.

It is important that the options are sorted out correctly. If they are wrong, it may mean that students find there is not enough equipment for them in certain classes, or they may be 'double-booked' for some classes. Computers can help schools to work out the options. They can do much of the tedious work involved in sorting out the information efficiently and reliably. Fig. 8.1 shows an options program in use.

Fig. 8.1 The 'Options' program in use

The J.R.R. Tolkien Comprehensive School

Hobbit Lane,
Smallville,
SM1 9QT.
Telephone 953875

Dear Parent,

From next September your son/daughter will be in Year Four. This year is the start of courses leading to GCSE examinations.

In Year Four, all pupils have to study some subjects like Maths and English. They have the chance to choose the rest of their subjects from several option groups.

The School has produced a book to help with the choosing of the Options and pupils are helped in tutor time. The choice of subjects has to be made from the list enclosed. The latest date for choosing is 31st May. Once the choice has been made please complete the form on the bottom of the list and send it to me.

The names of the subjects can be written in the spaces, and below this space is a box for the subject code. This year Mr. Snodgrass, our Head of Maths, is using the School microcomputer to help to sort out the options. The use of codes will help to speed up this part of the organisation.

Yours sincerely,

B. Baggins.

Bernard Baggins
Headmaster.

The Options

Here are the options which we will run next year.

A	B	C	D	E
Agricult. Sc AS	Geography GO	RE RE	Geography GO	History HI
Biology BI	History HI	Sociology SO	Sociology SO	History HI
Chemistry CH	Art AR	Art AR	Child Care CC	Biology BI
Physics PH	German GM	Chemistry CH	Computing CP	Basic st. BS
Integrated Sc. IS	Cooking HE	Child Care CC	French FR	Child Care CC
	Metalwork MW	Fabrics FA	Cooking HE	Computing CP
	Graphics TG	Music MU	Metalwork MW	Graphics TG
	Woodwork WK	Woodwork WK	Typing TY	Typing TY
		Typing TY		

✂ --

Options for Year Four

Put one subject in each box. Put the code in the small box below the option.

Name .... Class ....

Option A	Option B	Option C	Option D	Option E
Subject Cd	Subject Cd	Subject Cd	Subject Cd	Subject Cd

Fig. 8.2 This is how teachers collect information from parents about which options pupils wish to take for GCSE examinations

A computer file

The information put into the computer for the options at Tolkien School was put in one file. This file is like a file in the filing cabinet of Fig. 8.3. All the information in it is to do with options. The file is made up of records. Each pupil has a record, made up of seven parts or seven fields — name, form and five options. This arrangement of file/record/fields is the same in all data bases.

A computer helps to speed up the counting and sorting of files. It does not, on its own, make the files correct, as Mr Snodgrass found out when using the option program supplied with this book. Now read on . . .

Memo from the Head .... 1st June

Fred, Thanks for giving me the numbers in next year's options. Using the computer is much faster.
I see that one student has opted for Fabrics in option 2 and another one has chosen Physics in option 5. We didn't put these subjects in those options. What has happened? See me immediately!

B. Baggins

Fig. 8.4

Memo from Mr. Snodgrass ....

2nd June

Headmaster, You are quite right. The choices are not correct. The pupils you told me about filled out the forms incorrectly. I did not check them before they were put in and the computer was not programmed to either. Further checks have shown two dozen more mistakes due to incorrect typing of the data. We will have to do the options again with those students.

F. Snodgrass

sweat sweat

Headmaster

Fig. 8.5

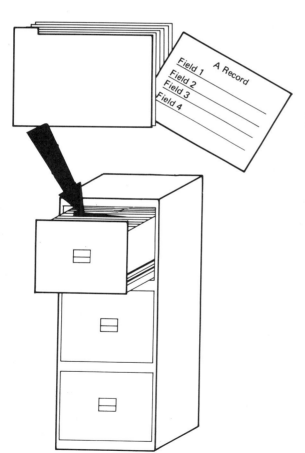

Fig. 8.3 A filing cabinet and the filing system

A Record
Field 1
Field 2
Field 3
Field 4

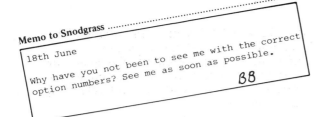

Memo to Snodgrass ....

18th June

Why have you not been to see me with the correct option numbers? See me as soon as possible.

BB

Fig. 8.6

Phone message for the Headmaster

2.00pm 19th June

Mrs Snodgrass phoned to say that her husband has been given a Doctor's note for sick leave for three months.

He has had a difficult time persuading the two dozen students who filled their forms in incorrectly to choose correct subjects. It has made him very run down. The final straw came yesterday when he spilt coffee all over the master data disc and then found that the baby had chewed his back-up disc. His wife found him lying on the floor chewing it too and muttering "Baggins, Baggins, Baggins..." before he collapsed. She says she will come to see you as soon as she can.

ACTIVITIES

Now its your turn to save Snodgrass. Try the following tests.

A1 Using the program **Options**, which accompanies this book, find out which two students chose their options incorrectly. Try to find out in the following ways:

(a) Select 'search the options' from the menu and pick the name field to select from. Press

RETURN

when asked what the field should contain. This will give you a complete list of all the options chosen. As they pass by, try to see who the two Students were.

(b) Select 'search the options' again. This time use field 4 and enter 'FA' when asked what the field should contain. The program will now do the hard work, and

you should easily identify the odd student. Do the same with field 7 and enter 'PH' for the other student.

A2 There is one other student in the data base whose options are completely wrong. Mr. Baggins did not find the incorrect student when he glanced through the list. Find out who the student is by using the program.

A3 Now produce lists for all the option groups in all five options and form lists of options for checking.

A4 Normal class sizes at Tolkien School are 30 for classroom subjects, 25 for science and 20 for craft. The smallest size of group that can be offered is 12. Look at your numbers and discuss how many groups should be allowed for each option. Which subjects should not be allowed because their numbers are too small? Should size be the only consideration?

Files in schools

Schools have been experimenting in other ways with computers. Here are a few of them.

School nominal roll

Every school has to have information about each student, ranging from basic details such as name, age and address to school reports, health matters and behaviour records. This information is stored on a file (Fig. 8.8) which is usually confidential.

Some of the information in your file (your name, age and form, for example) needs to be readily available. These details are not confidential. The collection of this basic information for all the people in one school is called the *nominal roll*. A typical nominal roll for a secondary school can be kept on paper, but schools are now using computers to store it. With the nominal roll on computer, it is easier to pick out and collect together information, for example about particular classes or year groups. Lists can be compiled quickly and accurately, and the nominal roll file can be used as a data base for other files such as for timetables or individually addressed letters.

Confidential information could also be stored on a disc, but it would be difficult to keep it confidential. In the future, school nominal roll information may be linked to big central computers at government offices. This will present problems if confidential information is also stored on school computers. How much of this information should be freely available, and who should be allowed to look at it?

Examination entries

Examination Boards which set, mark and award examinations use computers to handle all the information about entries.

It is important that the information which the boards receive is correct. To help this, some boards such as the Oxford Delegacy now allow schools to enter students using a computer data base (Fig. 8.7). The board supplied the school with a disc of programs necessary to create an examination entry

data base. Mistakes are still possible, for example if people don't check the information which is fed into the computer. With the correct details, processing all the entries is more accurate and reliable using a computer.

Form 7

Every country council must know each year how many students attend each school in their area. The numbers are grouped in a particular way e.g. students aged between 11 and 12, or students with birthdays on the 5th, 15th and 25th of each month. The numbers are then entered on a group of forms called *Form 7* .

Allocations of money and teachers to each school are based on the numbers from Form 7 and so it is important that the information is correct. Schools with the nominal roll on computer can use a computer program to present the information for Form 7. This makes counting up the numbers much easier and more efficient, although the original data base must be correct.

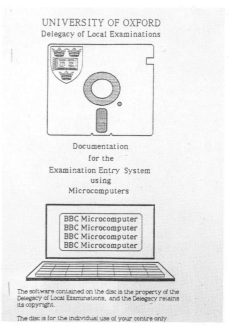

Fig. 8.7 This leaflet explains how to use the computer data base for examination entry supplied by the Oxford Delegacy

Files outside school

In schools, computers are helping to make the job of dealing with information easier and more accurate. If this is true in a small world like a school then it is even more true in the larger world outside school.

Mailing lists

Large companies use *mailing lists* to advertise their goods through the post (Fig. 8.8). These lists of names and addresses are stored on computer and used whenever there is a special offer to advertise. Your name will be added to a mailing list if you buy something that has a guarantee card, if you send off for a free offer or enter a competition.

Fig. 8.8 Examples of the junk mail that you may receive through the post

Bad debts

To buy goods on credit, you must be *creditworthy*, which means that people can rely on you to pay your debts. Many shops use credit checking agencies which keep the names of people who have been bad debts on computer databases. The agencies will check any name given to them by a shop against the bad debts list. If there is no record for that name on the database, then the person is a good credit risk.

The Data Protection Law

Using computer files to store information presents new problems concerning how to control access to the information (it is not always possible to look up computer files). Doctors, for example, are worried that patients' records stored on computer file will become available to people who should not see them.

ACTIVITY

Split up into pairs. One person takes the role of a doctor; the other person is a patient who is ill but is worried that the details of his or her illness will not be kept confidential. Try to work out how this situation can be overcome by discussing all the facts.

Many countries are concerned about the dangers of open computer files. Britain has a new law to protect information on files. This is the Data Protection Law. This law ensures that anyone who has information about people on computer will have to register with a *registrar*. The registrar will check that people can find out what the computer file says about them. If anyone disagrees with a particular database, then he or she can appeal to have the information changed. Some databases will be closed, police files or government files for example.

Examination Boards were worried that the law would force them to release examination results before they had been checked. Not only would this be misleading for the students, but it would waste the board's time and prevent them from getting the correct results out on time.

Most of these problems have now been resolved.

EXERCISES

1 What is a nominal roll?

2 What basic information does your school have about you?

3 How could the use of a computer speed up the running of a school?

4 Computers do not make mistakes. What are the three causes of mistakes in examination results and computer files?

5 What system does your school use to enter pupils for examinations? Does it use a computer or does it rely on a manual paper system? If a computer is already used, write a letter to the person in charge of exams explaining the pitfalls of using a computer for this task. If the system is a manual one write a different letter explaining how a computer could make examination entries easier to do.

6 Write a sentence to explain the meaning of each of the following:

(a) a mailing list;
(b) a bad debt;
(c) a computer record;
(d) a computer file;
(e) a filing cabinet.

7 Imagine that you are the parent of one of the two dozen pupils at Tolkien Comprehensive whose options were incorrect. You have been told that because of a computer error your child will have to be put into subjects that he or she has not opted for. However, another pupil has been told that the error was due to the computer but to Mr Snodgrass' mistakes. Write a letter of complaint to the Headmaster, Bernard Baggins, asking him to explain what the error was and how it happened. Tell him what you want him to do about it. Your letter could end by suggesting ways that such errors could be avoided in future.

TOPICS FOR DISCUSSION

D1 How much information contained in a school file should be put onto computer?

D2 How much information about students should be available to other people?

D3 You are in charge of a dentist's surgery. The dentist wants to use a computer to help with the running of the business. What will the computer do for the business? What files, records and fields would you advise the dentist to have?

D4 What are the advantages and disadvantages of being on a mailing list?

D5 You will soon be sitting public exams. Imagine that you sit down to your first exam and find that the questions are about something you have never studied. You will soon realise that you have been entered for the wrong exam. What should you do? Who is responsible for this error? Who is to blame for the error?

D6 Imagine that you start to receive through the post catalogues and brochures about all sorts of goods. You have not asked for them to be sent to you. Discuss why have they suddenly started to arrive. Try to decide what you would do if you wanted to stop them coming to you.

9
Computer crime

Comic strip: The Heist

Tracey and Sara go to the same school, and their interests lie definitely outside school. In the main they are interested in clothes, pop music and boys; in that order.

Sara's boyfriend, Rod, knows a lot about computers and he is trusted to use the school computer at any time. Much to Sara's disgust another girl, Anna, the class bully, starts paying special attention to Rod. Anna's brother left school some years ago and worked for a computer firm for a time until he was sacked for dishonesty. Encouraged by her brother, Anna starts using Rod's computer knowledge and the school's machine to rob various firms. Tracey and Sara discover them in the act. Their dilemma is, should they tell or should they join in?

Anna

Sara

Tracy

Rod

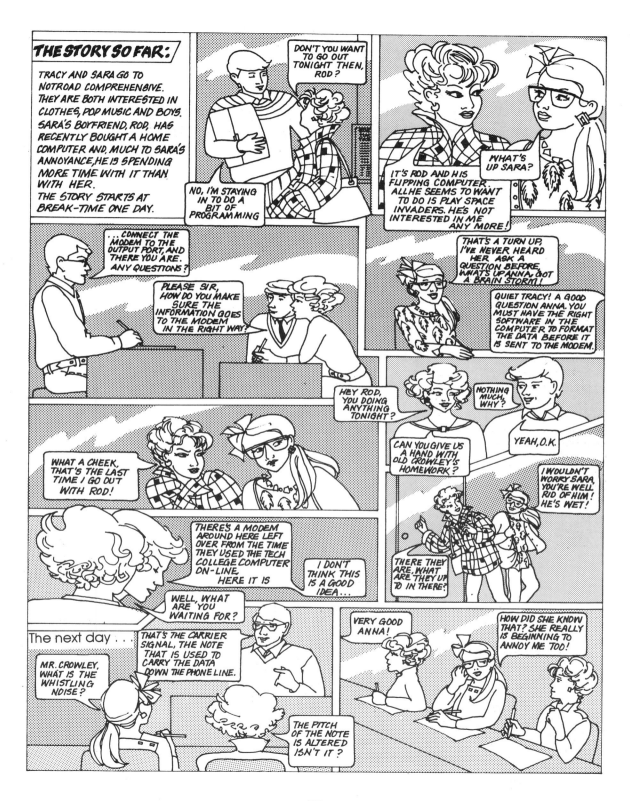

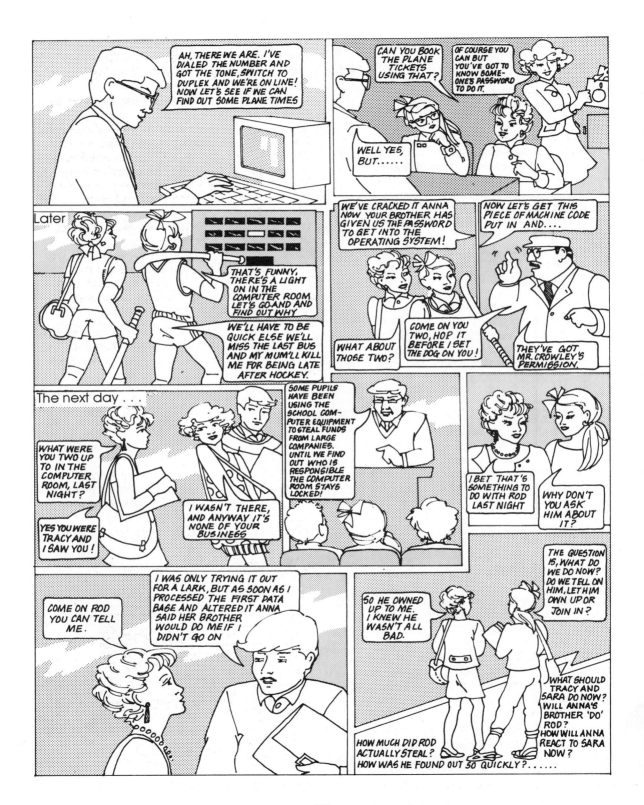

What does the story show?

There are several questions to be asked after you have read this story.

How realistic is the crime?

It is common for schools to own all of the technology in the story. Linking the modem, computer and phone lines together is no problem and may even be done already in schools that make use of a Prestel gateway. We have seen in other chapters that just making the connections is not enough. There are other things that have to be done before the hardware will link in with distant computers.

What else, beside the hardware, is needed to get onto a system?

The reference to Anna's brother is the key to this question. Once the phone connection has been made the users will have to prove that they are allowed onto the system. They will have to enter a password and probably an identification number. Anna's brother must have supplied this information in the story. In some places this sort of information is shared by an underground grape vine. Given his help and the school's equipment then the 'crime' is very possible.

Once you are on a system what can you do without getting caught?

The answer to this is that it depends on your knowledge of the computer system you have broken into. A novice will be detected very quickly in the same way as a novice burglar. Unlike a burglar it would be very easy for them to be traced once they had been detected.

How much longer will it be possible to get into systems in this way?

There will always be some systems that can be broken into but systems that are worth protecting (the ones that carry money and sensitive information) will become more difficult to penetrate as time goes on.

To understand how difficult or how easy it is to break into a system you need to look at the ways in which firms protect themselves from fraud.

New technology and crime

New technology has led to the development of new forms of crime.

Active crime uses technology to move money around illegally. It has been estimated that in America, direct access to a banking computer system would allow the thief to escape with 500 000 dollars at a time. The average armed hold-up makes only around 4000 dollars. Estimates for the cost of computer crimes in Britain vary, but figures of between 30 million and 2500 million pounds have been suggested. There are no definite figures because businesses are unwilling, and unable, to state exactly how much they lose.

One of the biggest worries for the banking world is that large robberies have already taken place undetected. If such a crime has occurred, then banks are likely to lose the trust of their clients, as well as the money.

Some people take pleasure in breaking into large computers systems without stealing from them. These 'hackers', as they are called, may then leave marks, 'electronic graffiti', to show where they have been. Removing such graffitti can be expensive and time-consuming.

Passive crimes are less complex than active crimes. A home microcomputer can be linked to the computer of a large company while the company is transferring information between its computers. Data

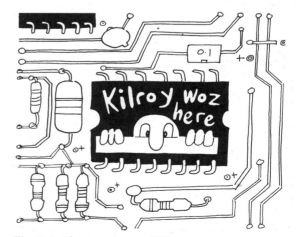

Fig. 9.1 Electronic graffiti?

such as financial reports or new product formulae would become available to the thief. As computer systems are used increasingly to hold information about people, it is worrying to think that such information could be leaked.

Security methods

Data stored in a computer system must be protected not only while it is within a particular building, but also during transmission to another system.

Within one building, complicated security arrangements can surround the hardware (just as valuables and money are protected in a bank). People working on the system may have restricted access to it — each person may understand only a small part of the system, and he or she may be allowed to perform only certain specified tasks. Access can also be protected by each operator using an identity card (Fig. 9.2) and an identity code which must be entered correctly before the computer will open up.

Fig. 9.2 This card reader is used to protect the computer system from unauthorised use

Data being transferred by telephone or by radio is more difficult to protect. Telephone lines can be intercepted easily and radio transmissions can be picked up. Coding data as it is transmitted is one way of protecting it, but the code must be agreed by both the sender and the receiver. The codes used often involve a shifted alphabet so that, for instance, every 'B' would be written as 'A'. A simple program for producing code shifted by any number of letters is listed in Fig. 9.3.

The power of these and similar security arrangements is often that they themselves are kept secret.

```
10 INPUT"HOW MANY LETTERS SHIFT",shift
20 INPUT"PRINT YOUR MESSAGE  AND PRESS RETURN",A$
30 D$=""
40  FOR N%=1 TO LEN(A$)
50    B$=MID$(A$,N%,1):REM TAKES A LETTER AT A TIME
60    IF B$=" " THEN 130:REM IGNORES ANY SPACES
70      C=ASC(B$):REM CONVERTS LETTER TO ASCII
80      C=C-shift:REM SHIFTS ASCII BY REQUIRED AMOUNT
90    IF C<65 C=90-65+C:REM WRAPS AROUND FROM A TO Z
100   IF C>90 C=65+C-90: REM WRAPS AROUND FROM Z TO A
11    D$=D$+CHR$(C):REM BUILDS GROUPS OF FOUR NEW
LETTERS
120    IF LEN(D$)=4 THEN PRINT D$+" ";:D$="":REM
PRINTS GROUP OF FOUR AND RESETS
130  NEXT N%:REM LOOPS UNTIL END OF MESSAGE
140 PRINT D$:REM PRINTS LAST FEW CHARACTERS
150END
```

Fig. 9.3 A simple program for coding messages

Breaking into the system

In the story at the start of this chapter, the passwords and identity codes were supplied by an ex-employee of the company. In real life, key information is not so easy to come by. You would not get any useful information if you telephoned a bank and asked for the passwords to their computer system. However, deception has been known to work. There has been at least one case of 'breaking and entering' a County Council Computer where the thief did just ring up the computer room, ask for the codes, was given them and proceeded to write rude messages all over the operating system. Some places are more conscious of security than others. In most commercial computer installations bluff would not work. The passwords that protect systems are set up by the users of the system. It is quite possible that a knowledge of the users would give a clue as to their passwords. A husband may use his wife's name, date of birth or his own middle name. If the system is not designed to stop a thief trying name after name eventually he or she will find a first name that works as a password.

Fig. 9.4 *One way of intercepting data!*

The thief who wants to intercept data and change it while it is moving along the phone lines needs access to the lines and a way of decoding the data. The first of these means entering a secure building and planting a bug. Secondly he or she will need to work out how to decode the code. Without knowing how many letters the code has shifted this could be difficult. It is not as difficult as it may seem, however. The frequency of letters in the coded message can be counted, and the frequency of the letters in the original language used can be counted. Knowing the frequency of the letters in a sample of the coded message and the frequency of the letters in the language used, it is possible to match letters with their codes and so to get the shift. A simple computer program would give a good guess of the letter shift. The thief then has a fast way of decoding the message.

Weak links

The way that a thief breaks into a computer system is no different in principle from the way in which thieves have always worked. There will be one part of the system that is easier to attack than any other. Once the weak link has been spotted the criminal uses it for his or her own gain.

Example 1
The weak link in the chain of communication is sometimes where the technology links up with people, and sometimes where it links with other technology. Crimes that have been detected show this.

A large American bank was robbed by a thief who found a weak link in its system. The thief realised that the slips of paper on the counter of a bank that were used for paying money into any account were the same size and colour as his own paying-in slips except they did not have on them his

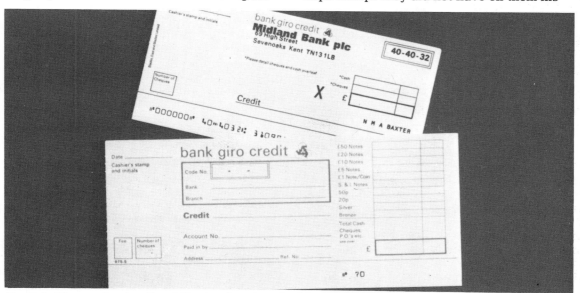

Fig. 9.5 *The paying-in slip at the top is printed with an account number. Any money paid in on this slip goes into the account. The slip at the bottom can be used by anyone. The account to be credited must be filled in*

account number in magnetic ink. He visited several branches of the bank and substituted his paying-in slips, (see Fig. 9.5), for the general-purpose ones. He relied on the cashiers not realising that the slips were different. As soon as other customers paid in money on his slips, the computer system placed that money in his account even though both the person paying the money in and the cashier thought that the money was going somewhere else. The computer was programmed to read the magnetic ink characters only. The thief then closed the account and disappeared.

Example 2

One of the reasons why it is difficult to break into remote computer systems is that the firms owning computers do not make the telephone numbers of their computers public knowledge. Hackers in America have realised for some time that the first link in the communication, the phone line, can be made to work for them and actually help them find computers.

What they have done is this. They have connected their home computers to the local telephone network. They have then written a program which tries every number and senses when the tell-tale whistle is present. The number is then noted as a computer line. The system can be investigated by the hacker at a later date.

Finding computer lines this way is slow and uses a lot of phone time. Phone charges are different in the States; local calls are not charged. Finding computer numbers by searching every number on an exchange is not a good idea in this country.

Example 3

There are several large banks in this country that give cashcards to their customers. This plastic card looks like a credit card. As you can see from Fig. 9.6, it has the number of the bank the name of the person who has the account, and the account number printed on it in raised letters. On the back of the card is a strip of magnetic tape with a personal code written on it. This code is secret and known only to the person who holds the account. When the card is put into a cash dispenser (Fig. 9.7) the machine reads the number on the back and the customer has to key in the number before any money can be given out. Thieves have realised that it is possible to

Fig. 9.6 *A cashcard like this allows you to draw money from your bank account even when the bank is closed*

Fig. 9.7 *These cash dispensers are in use all over the country*

read the data recorded on the magnetic strip using an adapted tape recorder. Using this sort of equipment it is also easy to alter what is recorded on the rear of the card. It is not so easy to record dummy codes since the banks have coded the codes! Increasing use of cashcards must mean an increase in fraud which uses the weaknesses of technology.

Example 4

Games software used on home computers is protected by copyright, as books are. The games are, however, easy and cheap to copy. Although this is illegal, copying is taking place more and more frequently. Software piracy is, in the end, self-defeating. It will lead to a decline in the amount of software being published. Software houses have to sell a certain number of games in order to keep going. As more games are illegally copied, so fewer games are sold. If you want to enjoy new computer games then don't take illegal copies — go out and buy the real thing.

Software houses have taken some precautions against copying, but these precautions must be kept secret if they are to succeed. One magazine was recently prosecuted for publishing details of how to overcome a security method used by Acorn computers. The magazine had to pay £65 000 pounds in damages. Similar amounts have been paid by businesses found using software illegally.

ACTIVITIES

A1 The computer program **Hacker**, which accompanies this book, will give you an idea of the way in which hackers have to work in order to break into a computer system. There are several stages.

(a) The telephone number of the system has to be found. Several years ago in London there were illegal telephone numbers which allowed students to make free telephone calls all over the world. These numbers had been set up by engineers. The information was leaked and spread around student London. In a similar underground way the phone numbers of computers are being spread. The phone number for this simulation is well-known to anyone who watches television.

(b) Passwords and identification numbers have to be known. In this simulation the form in which the date is entered has to be correct. The identification code depends on the date too. When you need it, you will find your password in this chapter.

(c) The data transmitted by the computer, when it finally believes that you are an authorised user, is in coded form too. The hacker will have to use some sort of decoder to break that code.

(d) To alter the data inside the system a knowledge of the computer is needed. The program is protected in the same way as the data in a real computer system. The computer will sound a siren if a mistake is made. Breaking into the program is not easy, in the same way as breaking into data is not easy. Finding the passwords from the program directly is not possible.

The final reward for pupils finding the correct answer should fit their crime. Perhaps they should do as the computer commands them!

A2 Hacking is not a game to be encouraged. It is not only expensive but it is also antisocial. Nevertheless, few adults realise that it does happen. Some questions put to people who work with computers will show how much they are aware of the possibilities. Ask people you know who work with computers the following questions.

(a) Does your computer need a password before anyone can use it? Does it need a key to unlock it?

(b) Does the password change often?

(c) How safe are the discs or tape? Are they locked up when they are not in use or can they be found sometimes lying on a desk?

(d) How often has the computer been broken into?

(e) When the service engineer calls does he show his identity card?

(f) If the computer can be linked to other computers by phone how many people know the phone number?

(g) Is there a record, kept by the computer, of who uses the computer?

The answers you get will be interesting. Share them in class and see what patterns come out. You will find that some firms are completely unaware of the dangers of computer crime. Other firms will be much more aware. How does your own school cope with the possibility of computer crime involving its own records? If your school uses a computer to hold information ask secretary in your school office the questions above.

EXERCISES

These questions can either form the basis of discussion or be answered on paper.

1 What is a hacker? What equipment is needed to be one and what information do you need to be successful as a hacker?

2 What is the purpose of a password?

3 If you were telling people about a new computer system what would you tell them not to do when they were making up their passwords?

4 Why do companies which employ computer staff pay them well?

5 Why are programming staff sometimes not allowed to write data on systems they program?

6 Why are programmers sometimes given parts of a large program to write?

7 The cost of computer crime in this country is only estimated. Why is it not possible to work it out accurately?

8 What is the difference between active and passive computer crime? Why are they both dangerous to individuals?

9 'Codes are used when transmitting data over a phone line or radio but all they buy is time.' Explain what is meant by this statement.

10 Code the following short message into groups of four using shifts of (a)4 and (b) − 2 letters:

THE COMPANY IS ABOUT TO CALL IN THE RECEIVER SELL YOUR SHARES RIGHT AWAY

11 Which of the two lines below is probably a coded message? Why did you choose it?

(a) DASD FGHT TOEP SLKK FHDU DPGI

(b) SSSS RTYY IOUT TTJG FHDD DASS

12 Try to decode the line you thought was a coded message in the last question.

13 Write a newspaper article called 'The crime of the century' in which a thief makes use of a computer.

14 How would you tell if a computer which your doctor uses is secure? Write a list of questions you would ask her or him to satisfy yourself that it was secure.

15 Write a suitable caption for the cartoon in Fig. 9.8.

Fig. 9.8

10
Games: from Monopoly to Space Invaders

Cuttings from the Smallville Echo

Schoolboy whizz-kid makes his fortune

14 year old Dick Bungle has more money than he knows what to do with. He is one of the new generation of computer experts that have made their marks and fortunes in the world of computer software.

Dick, who attends the Tolkien School, Smallville, was given his first computer at the age of eight. Since then he has progressed to bigger and more powerful machines. On his computer he wrote the enormously successful 'Attack on Moonbase Beta/Gamma'. This game proved so popular that Dick bought out the company that origiinally published it.

Dick's present fortune is estimated at around £300,000. He estimates that his income amounts to one pound for every minute of the day. Go to it Dick!

Local residents to press for Arcade's closure

Local residents, led by Mr. F. Snodgrass, a well known teacher, are pressing Smallville council to withdraw the license granted to Arcade owner Mr. D. Fender. The residents claim that the arcade on Scotland Road has become a nuisance. Mr Snodgrass made the following comments when asked about the Arcade:

"The Arcade has become a haunt for local youths. There is a lot of poor behaviour, shouting and litter around it. It is noisy and attracts trouble. When pupils truant from school we often find them playing in the Arcade."

The council meets in a week's time to consider the closure of the Arcade. Mr. D. Fender was not available for comment.

Teenager steals to play games

A thirteen year old boy was found guilty yesterday at Smallville juvenile court of stealing from a neighbour. He was sentenced to 48 hours community service, placed on probation for two years and ordered to repay the stolen money.

The boy, who attends a well known local school, broke into the house of a neighbour, 78 year old Mrs Smith, and stole a cash box from under her bed. The box held Mrs Smith's savings which amounted to £55.

The boy, who has not been named, claimed that he had to have the money in order to play the computer games in the local amusement arcade. When asked to comment after sentence had been passed he said:

"Well you get bored, don't you? I go down the arcade most lunch times but your dinner money don't go very far, do it? I just borrowed the money. I was going to give it back. If it hadn't have come from her I'd have got it from somewhere else."

The headlines show the two different sides of computer games. A few people have made money through the games industry, and some people have become addicts. There are groups of people in this country and abroad that are worried about the games craze. This chapter shows where computer games have come from, the types of games that are played now, the pleasures people get from these games and the fears for the future.

Computer games: what are they?

If you look at ancient Greek and Roman games, you can see the basis for some of today's games and sports. Running, shot-put and javelin are examples of ancient sports we still practise. Other sports — such as the more barbaric Roman games (often resulting in the death of one or both of the contestants) — have not been continued. All the games and sports we play today have four things in common with the ancient 'games': they allow a release of tension and energy; they provide a means for learning new skills; they are enjoyable for spectators; and they are also a good way of meeting people. These four qualities make games an important leisure activity. Computer games are simply a new development of these qualities.

The development of computer games

Video games first became available when integrated circuits were produced relatively cheaply and on a large scale. At first, the video games machines were large and expensive and found only in amusement arcades. They provided simple tennis simulations as Fig. 10.1 shows. Games like this are simple, but they do involve some skill and fast reactions. They soon beame very popular and variations on the basic game were developed.

With more sophisticated technology came the introduction of *games consoles* which are simple microcomputers with a power supply, joystick and control switch. The programs used on the games consoles were bought on a ROM chip in a plastic cartridge. When the cartridge was connected to the machine, the game could be played. These consoles were similar to the home microcomputer. As microcomputers became cheaper, a market developed for home games software. Sir

Clive Sinclair's ZX80 was the first cheap microcomputer and it now has not only a large amount of software written for it, but hardware adapters to connect games joysticks to the system (Fig. 10.2). Home computer games are now very similar to those in the amusement arcades. The arcade games machines are now similar to the home micro. The two markets have merged.

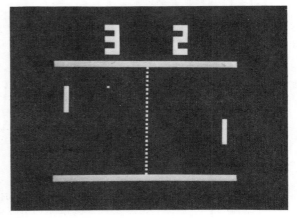

Fig. 10.1

Fig. 10.2 *A joystick connected to a Sinclair Spectrum. This makes the computer rather like an arcade machine*

Examples of computer games

Here are some comments on games from people who play them.

Snapper

This is what Sarah has to say about snapper-type games, as in Fig. 10.3,

'Snapper's alright, but it isn't very difficult. You can soon work out the way the little bugs move around the screen. You've got to keep clear of them unless your man has eaten a power pill and then the best thing is to chase the bugs.

It's mostly a question of physical skill with the keys. You don't need much thought. What makes it good is the graphics — they're really smooth.'

747 Simulator

Andrew, has this to say:

'Simulator (Fig. 10.4) is a difficult game. There are many controls which you have to remember and it takes quite a bit of skill to operate them properly.

There's fairly good graphics although the picture outside the window doesn't move very fast.

You have to understand how a plane works and a little bit about navigation. You've got to be able to think of yourself in the sky and to work out how to get to where you want to go. Its quite thoughtful'

Chess

Adrian's comments on chess:

'I've played chess for three years now and I still cannot beat the computer on its highest skill setting. It plays a good game although if you get it on the run by attacking, all it does is defend.

You don't need any physical skill, other than very simple button pushing, to get the game to go. The graphics are quite good; the movements are smooth because they don't have to happen fast.

Fig. 10.3 'Snapper'

Fig. 10.4 '747 Simulator'

Fig. 10.5 'Chess'

What makes a good computer game?

Here is a list of the features which Sarah, Adrian, Andrew and their friends thought make a good game. Perhaps you could add to the list.

A good game is one that:

1 has good colour graphics;
2 has lots of detail;
3 always has another surprise left;
4 has smooth animation;
5 uses any sounds well;
6 needs a lot of aggression;
7 requires practice to master it;
8 gets faster with higher scores;
9 needs a bit of thought to work out the best way to play it;
10 doesn't crash.

The disadvantages of home computer games

The quality of a home computer game may depend on the hardware itself as much as on the software used. For example, to produce colourful graphics lots of detail and several screens, a large memory is necessary. The most colourful displays on the BBC micro use ⅔ of the memory, which leaves little room for the program itself. As the sophistication of the software is restricted by the size of the memory, home computer games at the moment are unlikely to have all the qualities of a good game.

What's ahead?

Computer games have come a long way from the original repetitive tennis-type video games. The advance in hardware has a lot to do with this progress. One exciting prospect due to the improved power of the microcomputer is the possibility of 3-D games (Fig. 10.6).

The cinema, as long ago as the late '50s, has experimented with 3-D films. The 3-D effect was made by filming the scenes either using two film cameras mounted side by side and separated by a small distance or by using twin systems of lenses. The two films were projected on top of each other on the cinema screen, each through different coloured filters, as in Fig. 10.7. People watching the film were given cards with red and green filters mounted on them through which they watched the film. Each eye received a slightly different picture, as it would in real life, and a 3-D effect was achieved.

An identical method is possible using a small colour microcomputer. The scenes are programmed so that for each picture there are two overlapping pictures in red and green drawn in the correct perspective. The monitor screen would then give a 3-D picture if seen through red and green glasses.

Programs have already been written using this principle and more are likely.

The use of colour has made more realistic animation possible, as well as 3-D scenes. Along with increased memory, this technological advance will make games faster, more lifelike, longer lasting and more sophisticated.

People's tastes in games are also changing. There is an increasing demand for adventure game programs where the player is in the position of an explorer. On the route to a hidden treasure, the explorer must tackle various emergencies. These games

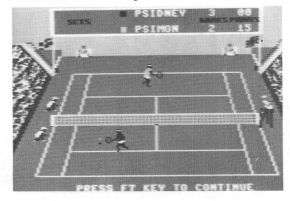

Fig. 10.6 This 3-D colour tennis game from Psion can be played on a microcomputer. The use of colour and smooth motion makes it very realistic

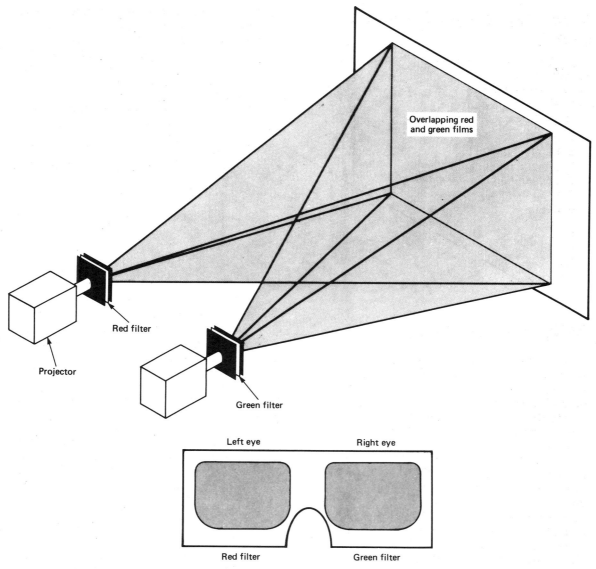

Overlapping red
and green films

Red filter

Projector

Green filter

Left eye

Right eye

Red filter

Green filter

Fig. 10.7 How a 3-D film works

involve chance, thought and skill — making them very exciting. A development from these adventure games is games combined with a book. Games like this require concentration and skill, so they do not suit everyone.

The next generation of computers offers great things to the world of computer games. Greater memory sizes, faster computers and more intelligent languages will mean games that are more and more life-like and convincing. For example, in the USA games arcades that put the players in a real situation are opening. Each player is dressed in 'space armour' and is armed with a 'laser'; both the armour and the laser are computer-controlled. The players fire their weapons at each other and the armour registers hits. When a player is hit, the laser is inactivated and he or she loses the game.

The final chapter of this book looks at the next generation of computers in more detail.

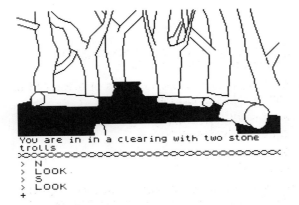

Fig. 10.8 A screen dump from 'The Hobbit'.
This is an exciting game that combines
strategic challenges with Tolkien's story

Fig. 10.9 Losing to a computer can be
frustrating

Fears about computer games

There is a growing feeling that computer
games are a danger to some people. Earlier
in this chapter four characteristics of games
were described. If we look at these
characteristics again, and ask 'do computer
games allow the players to experience this?'
the answer is not always 'yes'.

**Do computer games allow people to get rid of
their aggression?**
Computer games do make use of people's
aggression. Many games are fantasies based
on war themes, with the object of shooting or
killing the enemy. They certainly need the
player to become excited and aggressive.
Unlike some traditional physical games they
do not allow the players to use their bodies to
get rid of these tensions. The fear is that
computer games will get the players excited
without allowing them to release their
energy.

Do computer games develop skills?
Computer games do develop skills. They
make the players better at coordinating eye
and finger movements, although these skills
are not particularly useful. They do not help
to develop the total coordination developed
through playing traditional physical games.
The fear is that players who use computers
and never play traditional sports will not
develop their other muscles.

**Do computer games make good spectator
sports?**
Computer games do not make good spectator
sports. Usually, the crowd around the
computer game are there waiting to take
their turn. They are not very interested in
the person or people playing.

**Are computer games a good way of meeting
people and sharing experiences?**
Computer games are possibly a good way of
meeting people. The fear here is that people
will sit in front of a monitor, eyes glazed, for
hours on end without ever talking to anyone.

A disturbing picture can be drawn from
these comments on computer games. People
who spend most of their time playing
computer games and doing nothing else are
likely to be weak, badly coordinated, and
un-employable, social outcasts who are
constantly kicking the cat to get rid of their
frustrations. This is an overstatement. No
one is that obsessed; no one plays computer
games and never talks to other people, but
there are cases at colleges in this country of
teenagers becoming so obsessed with
computers that they sit up all night
programming and playing games. These *code-
junkies* as they have been called, have ended
up failing their exams. It has happened. Is it
going to happen to you? Perhaps instead of
playing computer football you ought to go out
and play the real thing!

EXERCISES

1 Make a list of ten computer games you have played. For each one award a mark out of ten for each of the following qualities:
- (a) animation;
- (b) graphics;
- (c) thought required;
- (d) skill required;
- (e) value for money;
- (f) use of sound;
- (g) amount of aggression needed;
- (h) amount of detail;
- (i) use of colour;
- (j) amount of practice needed;
- (k) reliability – does it crash?

Now add up the total for each game and sort the games into order – the ones with the highest total at the top. These are the ones which you enjoy most. Does your order match that of your friends?

2 What are the four reasons given in the chapter why people enjoy playing games?

3 Which of these four reasons still apply to computer games? Which one applies least to computer games?

4 What are the three types of game referred to in the chapter?

5 Write down two examples of each of the three types of game.

6 Describe in writing a game that involves all three types of game.

7 What does your family think of computer games?

8 Write down what you think are the main dangers of playing computer games.

9 Write down the four main attractions which computer games hold for you.

10 Games can be used to teach many skills. Choose a skill you are good at and design a computer game that attempts to develop this skill. You don't have to be a programmer to do this.

11 Describe Dick Bungle's 'Attack on Moonbase Beta/Gamma'.

12 Write your own reviews of the programs that go with this book. Use the headings given in the chapter (graphics, sound etc.) to help you to describe the programs.

TOPICS FOR DISCUSSION

D1 What do you think of Dick Bungle?

D2 Split into groups of four. Decide who is going to be Mr. Snodgrass, Mr. D. Fender, the youth convicted of theft and Dick Bungle. Now discuss whether the Arcade should stay open or not. If your school has a video recorder and camera it would be a good idea to film the best group for all the class to see.

D3 Which non-computer game would you most like to see programmed and why?

D4 What changes would you make to the design of computer games and the computers they are played on to change the games into spectator games?

11
Artificial intelligence

ACTIVITY

Try the following simple tests in pairs. As one of you does each test, talk about how you are doing it. The other person should make notes about how the problem is being solved.

1 What is the missing number in this set:
1 2 4 7 11 ? 22 29.

2 What is the missing letter in this set:
W E ? C O M E.

3 Which of the parts A to D of Fig. 11.1 should be added between 3 and 4 to complete the sequence.

4 Which of the following is the odd one out:

stairs room garage car lorry.

5 Try to answer the following question.
It took one man three days to fill a bath with water from a well, using a bucket. After he had gone, three men using three buckets tried to fill the same bath. How long did it take them?

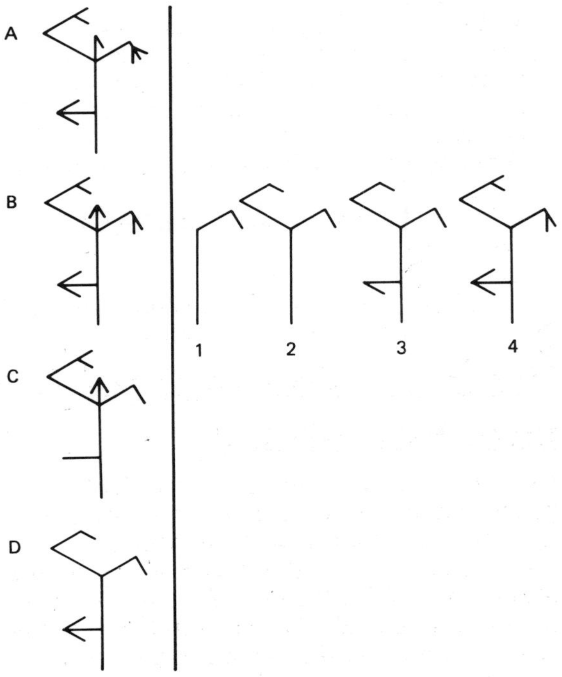

The answers to the first three questions in the activity are easy. Questions 4 and 5 are not so simple.

Fig. 11.1 The intelligence test, question 3

What is intelligence?

A discussion of the topic of artificial intelligence has to start with an explanation of what intelligence is in man. The way you solved the simple problems in the activity is a demonstration of intelligence. How did you solve the problems? Talk it over in class with your friends and the teacher. You probably used the sorts of methods described below.

1 'I saw that there were a load of numbers and that they were getting bigger. I counted the difference between each number and worked out that the number after 11 had to be 5 bigger than 11 and 6 less than 22. This means the number is 16.'
What sort of knowledge does this problem need to solve it?
2 'I saw straight away that the word should be 'WELCOME', so the letter missing is 'L'.
What sort of knowledge does this problem need to solve it?
3 'I looked at the pictures and saw that each branch of the tree was getting one more twig each time, so the answer must have one more twig than the picture before it.'
What sort of knowledge does this problem need to solve it?
4 'All of the words have one letter twice except 'car'.'
Or
   'All of them have doors except "stairs".'

What sort of knowledge does this problem need to solve it?
5 'One man took three days so three men would take one third of the time.'
Or
   'The bath was full already, so they would take no time at all.'
What sort of knowledge does this problem need to solve it?

A lot of knowledge is brought together to solve even the simple problems above. In questions 4 and 5 there are several ways in which the knowledge can be put together; the different ways give different answers. When 'intelligence' is discussed, it usually means the way that people put together the knowledge, as well as the knowledge itself. Someone who has great intelligence can put together ideas in new and exciting ways.

Intelligent computers would be easier to work with. Computers that have artificial intelligence will be able to understand speech and writing, and it will be possible to solve problems using them without first programming and without having to type in the questions. Artificial intelligence is the science that is trying to make computers think in the same way as you did when you were doing the questions — solving problems by recognising patterns. Artificial intelligence means computers working out the answers.

Problem solving: pattern recognition and common sense

How do we solve problems? We look at the problem until parts of it look as if they link up with each other or with situations which we have met before. We then incorporate the observations from the problem into a known pattern and try this new pattern to see if it is right. The answer then becomes part of 'common sense' that could be used to answer new problems.

Problem solving, the sign of intelligence, means being able to recognise patterns. Humans are particularly good at seeing patterns, and at hearing them. The senses of touch, taste and smell are also able to distinguish patterns but it is not possible to tell so much from them without training. Senses can be trained to see patterns. In the same way, people can be taught to see patterns and so to improve at solving problems. Their intelligence will be developed.

Researchers into artificial intelligence believed that if intelligence could be developed in humans then the same could be true of computers. After all, they argued, computers have several advantages over human beings. They are much more accurate; the speed at which they operate is much greater; they do not tire; they do not forget and they can be programmed to do anything. Most important of all — computers do not have the prejudices that humans have. Artificial intelligence may help us solve a lot of problems and it may help society in other ways. For example, new works of art and music could be developed by the intelligent computer. Computers have not been developed far enough for these possibilities to be achieved. The reason for this lies in the way that the computer is built compared to mankind. The problem is the software, the way that computers are programmed to work and also the hardware, the computers themselves. Some pictures will help to show up these two problems.

Some patterns that are not all they seem

Fig. 11.2 is a drawing of a cube. The drawing is called a *wire frame* because all that is drawn are the lines that make up the sides. The cube could be made up out of lengths of wire. Quite a simple cube — or is it? Some of you will see one cube and others will see another. Fig. 11.3 shows the two cubes that will be seen. In one, the cube is being viewed from above; in the other case, the cube is seen from underneath. If you look back at the first drawing (Fig. 11.2) you can now see both drawings as your viewpoint flicks between them. What you see depends on the viewpoint. You can see both types of cube in a single drawing because you have not been given enough information to decide from what angle the drawing is taken.

Fig. 11.4 is another well-known drawing. The lines show the outline of both a candlestick and two faces. The shading in Fig. 11.5 shows up the two different ways of seeing the picture. There are many more simple tricks of the eye and brain. A collection of them can be seen in the Science Museum in London. In all of the cases you will see things that are not there because the information you have been given is not sufficient.

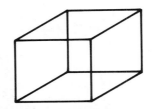

Fig. 11.2 A wire frame cube

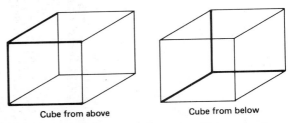

Cube from above   Cube from below

Fig. 11.3 The cube can be viewed in one of two ways, depending on which corner is allowed to stick out. The lines on these drawings have been thickened to show up the two ways clearly

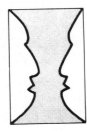

Two faces or a candlestick?

Fig. 11.4 Two faces or a candlestick?

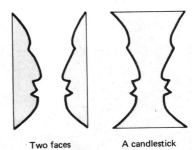

Two faces   A candlestick

Fig. 11.5 The shading has been altered in these two drawings to indicate the two pictures that could be seen in the one picture in Fig 11.4

Fig. 11.6 'Waterfall' by M.C. Escher

Fig. 11.6 includes much more information than the previous two pictures. Even so, there is something wrong with it. It was drawn by an artist called Escher in 1961 and it is entitled 'Waterfall''. There is plenty of information for the eye and brain to take in when looking at the scene; the building is solid; the fields in the background are terraced in a way that you might see in Europe; the woman hanging out her washing is natural enough. What is wrong with the painting is the direction of the water flow. If you have not seen the impossibility of its course, then follow the water from the waterfall. It goes round in a complete circle and on its way it manages to drop down the waterfall perhaps seven or eight metres. This means that it must be going back uphill from the bottom of the fall to the top again. This, common sense tells us, is not possible. Even if the water wheel was some kind of pump, it still could not make the water flow uphill in an open canal. Esher's skill at drawing has been used to good effect. He has cleverly drawn all the angles of the building correctly and naturally. He has even shaded the walls and pillars to give strength to the picture. All of the background seems to be normal but what appears possible at first sight turns out to be completely impossible.

How surroundings help us see

In the Figs. 11.2 and 11.4 you could not make up your mind what you were seeing. The diagrams had too little detail surrounding them to give the extra clues that humans need to make sense of what they see and to make up the patterns on which analysis of the environment is based. In Fig. 11.6 the patterns were all normal, except for the passage of the water. Our experience of the world tells us that this behaviour is not quite right for water. So although most of the picture fits in with patterns that we recognise, our knowledge from outside the picture tells us that it is wrong. We are always making use of our understanding of the world and our experience of it. Humans have a world picture that helps to solve problems.

Vision is not just a question of eyes

Our eyes provide us with a visual image of the world around us, but processing this image involves our brain as well. The eye and the brain are linked by a system of nerves arranged in a fixed way which cannot be changed. This 'wiring' system allows pattern recognition — helping us to recognise patterns which we have seen before.

In making computers intelligent, we would have to provide them with a world picture and a wired processing system (as in the eye).

You now should understand the two major problems that we face in trying to make computers intelligent. These are the lack of wired processing and the lack of a 'world picture' in the computer to help it to fit what it is told to familiar patterns.

The third major problem

The third problem standing in the way of artificial intelligence is known as the combinational explosion. This can be explained by looking at the way computers can be taught to play chess.

It has been possible to produce computer programs that play very good chess games (Fig. 11.7). The programs work by giving points to moves and combinations of moves: the good moves have more points than the poor moves. Chess players have told the programmers which are good moves and which are poor moves. The programmers then write programs that set the computer up to consider all the moves possible from a particular position and to keep a running total of them. The computer then sorts all the moves into order and takes the one with the most points. This sort of program is top-down which means that the computer has been told of all the possible moves from a given position. The machine then selects the move with the most points; this is the best move at that point in the game. The program works because the rules deciding which ways in which each individual piece is allowed to

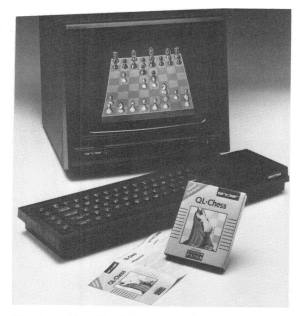

Fig. 11.7 *The Sinclair QL can be programmed to play a good game of chess. This 3D chess game is an advanced version that helps the user to learn chess strategy*

move are limited, although there are many ways of moving all the pieces.

In real life, things are not so simple. Look at Fig. 11.8. There are far more pieces in a factory than on a chess board and there are also many more ways in which these pieces can be moved around without breaking any rules. Mathematicians have shown that the combination of more rules and more pieces is so huge that it is impossible to produce for the real world the sort of programs that play chess. This *combinational explosion* has been used to prove that artificial intelligence is impossible.

Researchers in the artificial intelligence field claim that since it is possible for people to cope with this combinational explosion, despite their slow processing and small memory, then surely computers can overcome the problem. It is this belief that keeps people enthusiastic about artificial intelligence.

Fig. 11.8 *The inside of this factory is a complex place*

How far have we come?

In 1956 ideas about artificial intelligence and what it means were first developed. The test for intelligence, the *Turing Test*, was also invented.

This test is shown in Fig. 11.9. It involves a computer, two simple keyboards and two VDUs all linked together. An operator at one keyboard types messages in English and receives replies on the screen from the computer or from the other operator. If the first operator cannot tell which answers come from the computer and which come from the other operator, then the computer is said to be intelligent.

In 1961, NASA and other organisations sponsored research into artificial intelligence. Intelligent robots, like the one shown in Fig. 11.10, would be very useful for investigating space. Intelligent computers would also be valuable for analysing satellite pictures of the Earth.

The research produced simple robot systems for use in factories, but NASA withdrew their support as the research did not go as far as they had expected. The most significant development was made by a man called Winograd who produced a complex program allowing the control of a robot arm

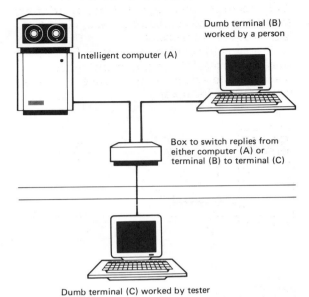

Fig. 11.9 The test of artificial intelligence requires the equipment shown here. The tester is linked either to a computer or to another human. If it is not clear from the messages received by the tester on the VDU whether he or she is linked to the computer or to the person, then the computer is said to be intelligent.

Fig. 11.10 The Russian moon surface vehicle that was used to investigate the surface of the moon

with a camera on it. The robot responded to commands typed in English and it would 'talk' about the tasks it was doing by printing sentences on the computer screen. Fig. 11.11 is a diagram of the system.

Attempts to develop this system further were unsuccessful. Despite many years' research into artificial intelligence, we have little to show for it yet.

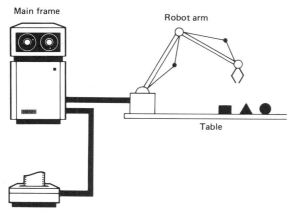

Fig. 11.11 *The experiments that Winograd put together allowed people to tell this computer, in English, what to do with the blocks on the table*

Where is artificial intelligence now?

In this country and in Japan there have been a number of developments that look as if they will make great changes quite soon e.g. Fig. 11.12. These developments have needed new machines and new programs. They are being improved all the time. Some examples of the use of artificial intelligence, or AI as it is known, are as follows.

Example 1
The giant Plessey company has joined up with universities in London, Edinburgh and Loughborough to produce a speech-driven typewriter. They hope to put together a machine that recognises the shape of spoken words and changes those shapes into typed words, without understanding what the words mean. Fig. 11.12 shows a similar system developed by IBM.

Example 2
A type of artificial intelligence is being used

to help or to replace people who have expensive knowledge and training. People like doctors and motor mechanics all need training and practice in order to do their jobs. Their skills have to be developed over a long time. The jobs they do can be vital, and if they are careless then lives are put at risk. The need for a system to help these people to make the right decisions is clear. The systems which have been developed are called *expert systems*. The use of an expert system should make a doctor's diagnosis more accurate; it may allow a semitrained person to get some idea of what is wrong with an ailing car.

Expert systems are made by putting together the skills of people like doctors, with those of a computer programmer. The expert has to tell the programmer how she or he works and the programmer then writes a program which uses that particular way of working to process all the knowledge about the subject. This knowledge is used as the data base for the computer.

In the activities section there is a chance to use a simple expert system to analyse your personality. This use of expert systems is being made in firms to help them when selecting people to fill vacancies.

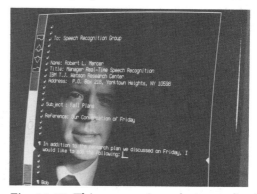

Fig. 11.12 *This screen is a photograph of a speech recognition system which IBM have developed*

The next step to AI

These three problems then, have, slowed the development of AI.

1 Lack of a 'world picture'. Today's computers are only fed the information that is needed to do a certain job. They 'forget' the information when they move on to a new job. They do not build up a large 'body of knowledge' which they can use to solve new problems.

2 No wired processing in present computers. The insides of today's computers are set up so that they can be programmed in almost any imaginable way. The human brain does not have this freedom; it is wired so that it can only work in certain ways.

3 The combinational explosion. In the real world the number of ways things can move and fit together is very large. It has been suggested that this number is so large that no computer can deal with it.

The standard plan of a computer going through its program one step at a time has restricted the development of AI in present computers. What is needed is a collection of processing computers that break down the

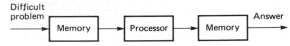

Fig. 11.13 (a) An ordinary computer works through the program step by step

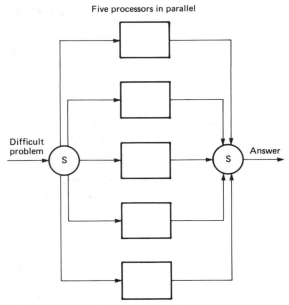

Fig. 11.13 (b) A parallel processor breaks each stage of the problem into several parts and deals with each part separately, but simultaneously.

program into parts. These parts can all be done at the same time. These computers are called *parallel processors* and are being developed in the Japanese search for the *fifth generation* (this is the name given to the next step in computing). Fig. 11.13(b) is a diagram of how parallel processing works.

As well as this new technology, AI computers will need to have certain ways of problem-solving built in. In the same way as the eye processes the information it receives before sending signals to the brain, parts of the computer will be wired to process information in one way only. Present computers lack this built in dedication.

Programs which are able to write other programs will need to be developed. This has already happened in a small way in businesses. For instance, *The Last One* is a business package that allows a businessman to set up a unique computer system. It is a collection of programs that prompts the businessman for information about the business and then writes the programs needed specifically for that business, according to rules that the authors have put into the package.

Different views of artificial intelligence

The issue raised by AI are far-reaching. AI will affect the way we live more than almost any other invention. There are some extreme views of what will happen when AI comes about.

View 1: AI will solve many of mankind's problems.

View 2: AI will be used by a few people to have power over others.

View 3: AI will develop rapidly and it will soon overtake mankind's abilities.

View 4: AI has already been developed. At the moment it is possible to switch it off, so it has kept a low profile. As soon as we hear that the independently thinking computer has been built it will be too late. The first thing that an independently thinking computer will do is protect itself from being switched off.

View 5: AI will mean that human experts will be redundant.

AI is likely to turn out somewhere between the first viewpoint and the other four. What do you think?

ACTIVITIES

A1 The program called **Profile** on the disc accompanying this book is a small expert system (Fig. 11.4). The program combines programming skill with a knowledge of personal qualities. It could be used by an employer to find out more about the people who have applied for a job. Some employers already use questionnaires to help them make up their minds who to employ. This example is taken from a questionnaire used by Inspectors of schools to help them to train and select Deputy Heads.

The knowledge that was used to make up the questionnaire supposes that there are eight personal qualities which can be easily measured in this way. There is a bank of 56 questions in the questionnaire and the person is prompted by sentences to say how strongly she or he feels about the way in which she is described by the sentences. After the 56 questions, the total score for each quality is given and a bar chart is drawn. The bars represent the eight personal qualities; the size of each bar reflects how much of each quality a person has. Run the program and answer the questions honestly. The eight qualities are as follows:

1 Ideas person or plant
This quality shows how good a person is at thinking up new ideas. Someone who is never stuck for something to do, who is good at making and creating things, and who breaks new ground will have a high score in this quality.

2 Chairman
A person who is strong in this quality will be someone who is a leader, and who is fair and listens to people. She or he will be a good judge.

3 Critic
This quality indicates how good someone is at seeing other people's shortcomings, and weaknesses. A high critic score indicates someone who will tell other people when they are wrong, without worrying about the consequences.

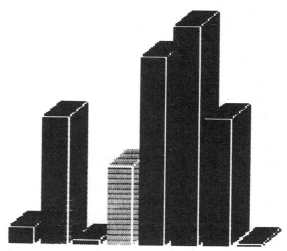

Personal Profile

Fig. 11.14 A screen dump from the program 'Profile'

4 Worker or implementer
This quality reflects how good someone is at making things work. Someone with a high score in this quality may not have new ideas, but he or she will make other people's ideas work.

5 Team builder
A high team-builder score indicates someone who is good with people. She or he is easy to get along with, surrounded by friends, and she would always be on hand when help was needed.

6 Shaper or unofficial chairman
A person strong in this quality will speak out when she feels that a friend is wrongly treated. She will be trusted by friends.

7 Contact or resourcer
This quality reflects how good someone is at finding out where to get something. A high score in this quality indicates someone who will always be able to 'fix you up, squire'.

8 Inspector
A person strong in this quality will be

good at doing things requiring care and patience. She or he will watch friends and offer help when they need it.

Does the result of your profile surprise you? Does it surprise your friends? It is more likely that the result you get is a good reflection of how you see yourself rather than how others see you.

A2 How do you solve problems?
The program called **Hacker** accompanying this book will help you to see how people solve problems. When you run this program use a cassette recorder to record all you say when you are trying to solve the problem. Listen to the tape and count up the number of times you speak a sentence. Try to decide which of the groups below the meaning of the sentence comes into:

1 sensible suggestion;
2 silly suggestion;
3 common sense;
4 special knowledge (e.g. a mathematical idea);
5 working out from 1, 3 or 4 above;
6 statements of opinion (e.g. "This is silly").

This activity should show you how good you are at concentrating (low numbers of groups 2 and 6); how often you use common sense (high numbers of group 3) and how important specialist knowledge is when solving problems.

EXERCISES

1 Copy and complete the following sentences by filling in the blanks.
(a) .... is the name given to machines that are programmed to .... for themselves.
(b) Some people think that computers can never be made truly intelligent because the possible .... of rules and actions in the real world are so large.
(c) Computers can be programmed to play intelligent games such as .... since the combination of .... and .... are limited.
(d) In order to play chess a computer has to be given a general .... of action. It awards .... to moves and makes the move with the highest number.
(e) Pattern .... in humans involves common sense which comes from .... of the world.
(f) Intelligent computers will need to have a .... view. This means a large .... as well as clever programs.
(g) Senses can be .... to recognise patterns.
(h) A wire frame drawing shows only the .... of a shape. The shape can be .... through.

(i) Visual tricks like Esher's .... rely on parts of the picture being correct. When the picture is viewed as a .... then it can be seen that the parts do not fit together in a known ....
(j) The Turing test of computer .... needs a human operator to be linked to another person and a computer. If the computer has .... then the operator would not be able to tell which of the two he or she is .... to.
(k) An .... system is the name given to a suite of programs containing the way in which an expert solves .... and a data base of .... of the area in which they work.

2 Describe how you think expert systems might be used in the following applications in order to improve the quality of the work done:
(a) teaching in schools;
(b) town planning;
(c) treating the sick;
(d) writing music;
(e) investigating crime.

3 Look carefully at the illustration Fig. 11.15. It is another of Esher's prints. What is wrong with the drawing? Describe how he has made the picture so realistic. How is the brain fooled into believing what it sees?

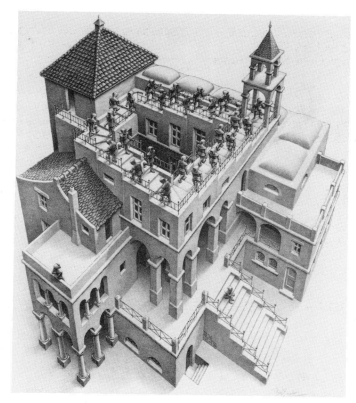

Fig. 11.15 'Ascending and Descending' by M.C. Escher

TOPICS FOR DISCUSSION

D1 The following is a list of some of the most difficult problems facing mankind. If artificial intelligence was finally created in which order should it tackle them — which is the most pressing problem?

famine; overcrowding in cities; warfare; overpopulation; pollution; space flight; disease; pest control.
Why did you choose that particular order? Which is the problem most likely to be solved by artificial intelligence?

D2 The idea that intelligent machines would treat mankind as a threat has been suggested. Imagine that you are one of the few remaining humans on Earth following a take-over by machine intelligence. What would you say to the machine to persuade it to keep you and the rest of mankind alive. Write out the dialogue.

D3 Choose two of the following occupations and discuss how artificial intelligence could make redundant people who now do these jobs:

doctor; nurse; teacher; TV repair man; garage mechanic; pilot.

D4 Artificial intelligence, when it is developed, will be the most powerful tool mankind has ever had. What rules need to be made now to make sure that this power is not misused? (There are three already mentioned elsewhere in the book.)

12
A look into the future

This chapter is a window on the future. Through it you will see some of the things that may happen in the next few years. When you read this chapter some of what you read may seem impossible. In a world that uses computers nothing that you read here is impossible. Some of it is happening now.

Changes in hardware

Developments in hardware

Size and speed

The new few years will see major advancements in the size and the operating speed of the computers which you find in schools, offices and factories today. A good guess is that machines with larger memories will be built for home and school within the next decade.

Hand-in-hand with the increase in memory size will come an increase in the processing speed. Present restrictions are largely the result of the way that integrated circuits are made today. These restrictions will be removed by making the circuits in other ways.

The patterns on the silicon chips in existing micros are drawn out using ultraviolet (UV) light. Experiments using other types of wave which draw finer lines are now underway. There is the possibility of using *ion beams* or a fine beam of electrons. Both of these ways will mean finer lines on the chips and so smaller circuits and faster computers.

New materials

Another development will be the use of artificial materials for the production of integrated circuits. Existing machines use silicon, gallium arsenide or other materials. A circuit is then made by building up layers of materials on top of the original material and etching away what is not needed. Future methods may start with an artificial sandwich of materials several layers thick. This will mean that circuits will be much deeper than at present, with as many as two dozen layers. The advantage of this is that many circuits present can be made together, which reduces the time taken to make them.

New hardware

Biochips

Biochips are a combination of computer technology and some material which reacts to changes around it. For example, certain chemicals react to the gases given off by explosives by making a complex pattern of electrical signals. Although this reaction is not as obvious as the change in colour which you have seen when litmus is brought into contact with acid, the principle of the indicator is the same.

Bomb-detecting biochips will make use of an outer coating of sensitive material to detect the presence of explosives. Inside this outer chemical layer is an integrated circuit that makes sense of the complex patterns of signals coming from the chemical and interfaces these to a microprocessor. The bomb detector would have a program contained in the *read only memory* (ROM) that controls the biochip and the microprocessor. The output of this device could be a simple light that flashes in the presence of explosives or a meter that gives an accurate measure of explosive concentration or strength.

More fanciful ideas that make use of bio-chip technology include the welding together of more complex chemical indicators that respond to chemicals in the blood stream or at any place in the body. Using the right indicator a direct interface between, say, the brain and a computer could be made. This would eliminate the need for any other type of interface, as the person would be in complete two-way communication with the computer. Such an individual would have immediate access to the power of the computer and through telephone links to all the data bases in the world. These ideas are a long way in the future but perfectly possible even with today's technology.

Interactive video
One development that is now taking place is the linking together of video and computer control. The new video disc players store the TV pictures on a plastic disc that is read by a laser and converted into a TV signal. The disc is not affected by scratches like an ordinary record disc and so it has a long life.

Within the next few years 'learning stations', built from a video disc player, a micro (with its own disc drive) and a monitor, will start to be used to teach people. The program loaded into the micro would control which still pictures and pieces of film are to be shown and in what order. Students would be able to control what is being shown and they will also be tested by the computer to see if they have understood the work. This new combination of hardware is called

High resolution colour monitor

Video disc player

Microcomputer containing instructions controlling the video disc player

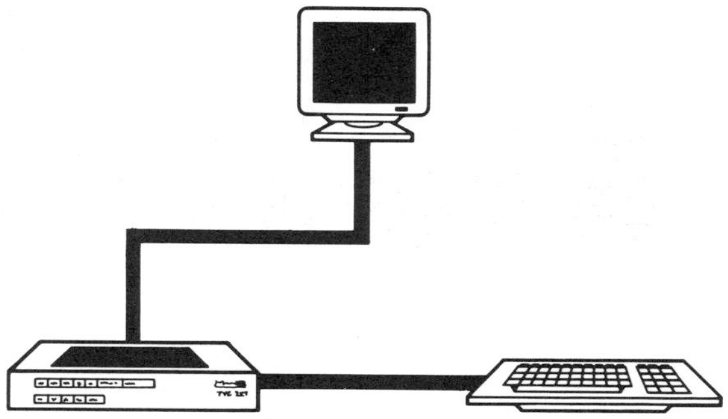

Fig. 12.1 Interactive video involves linking together a video disc player, capable of holding thousands of pictures, and a computer. The program in the computer controls the order in which the pictures on the video disc will be shown. The benefit of such expensive hardware is that many still and moving pictures, sounds and diagrams are stored on a small piece of plastic. The information is easy to retrieve and it can be shown in a clever and entertaining way

interactive video. Fig. 12.1 shows how the system is arranged.

Parallel processors
The final development in this section is *parallel processing.* Computers that contain more than one processor are already being used. The research and development work done into satellite and missile behaviour needs computers that can calculate very quickly. The most up-to-date computers involved in this work use parallel processors. These processors separate out the calculation into several parts that are done at the same time rather than one after the other, as in the more traditional computers. This way of working makes the computers very much faster. The human brain uses cells to store information. They are much slower than the smallest parts of a computer but the overall speed of the brain is much faster than a computer when solving some problems because the many cells deal with parts of the problem all at the same time. The next generation of computers, the fifth

generation, will almost certainly be built around an array of processors rather than around one central processor. This way of building computers will make them faster and so capable of solving more complicated problems faster.

Fig. 12.2 This computer, the Sinclair QL, combines many of the features of the next generation of computers. It can be made to 'multitask' (perform more than one job at a time) and it has a very large memory

Developments in software

The increases in size and speed of computers in the next generation will make possible some extremely exciting applications.

Multi-tasking

One such application that is used now, in a simple form, is *multi-tasking*. Multi-tasking means being able to run more than one program at the same time. This type of program will be seen on many office micros. For example, a typist may want to print a letter while editing another letter on the wordprocessor. The computer can be programmed to do both things at once. It works by dividing the memory in two and putting the programs and data for each job into one of the two parts. It then gets the computer to 'hop' between both parts.

Smart cards

Shoppers in the French cities of Caen, Lyon and Blois and students at one of the colleges in Paris have had the chance to try *smart cards* for some time (see Fig. 12.3). These cards look like credit cards but they have a microchip built into them. This chip acts as a memory just like the magnetic strip on the back of ordinary credit cards. Unlike these strips the chip can be 'written on' by another computer when they are linked together. The chip stores information about its owner.

Data links

There will be more electronic information coming into and out of homes in the next few years. These are *data links*. Already, home computers can be linked to other machines through Prestel. There are several services that also come into the house that could use the telephone line. Electricity and gas meters could both be read directly by the companies' computers. There would be no need for a meter reader to call and bills could be produced more accurately.

This mundane use for a data link is one of many possibilities. Using a home micro linked by telephone line to other machines, it will be possible to order and to pay for goods. Many information data bases will be available.

New languages

Leaping further into the future, programs will become more intelligent. Software engineers will have much more memory to use so that computers will be given common sense based on a large data base of everyday facts and situations.

Fig. 12.3 A smart card

Views of the future

Computer technology will change people's lives during the next few years but computers are not going to take over, however. Changes will happen slowly and in 'pockets'. For example, videos have been in some homes for several years but in other homes they have yet to appear. In a similar way, computer technology will appear in some places first. There will not be a sudden explosion of computers everywhere.

The speed of change will increase. When computers can understand speech and answer back they will seem very lifelike. When they are able to control cars, credit and communications they will be even more powerful tools. They will become easier to use and more people will want to use them. Despite their power and lifelike qualities computers will still be machine tools built to help people. Because they have been built by people they will make mistakes. Sometimes those mistakes will be obvious, but not always. In short, computers are only as good as the people who make and use them.

Fig. 12.4 The Ford 'Eltec' is a family car of the future. Its systems are all coordinated by a single sophisticated computer

ACTIVITY

The Factory

The Factory had been built on waste land near the railway. Its bleak, grey outside gave no clue to what was inside. No signs, neon or painted, hung over the one door. The few windows were small and set high in the walls so that no inquisitive eye could see in. The winds that swept down over the town from the moor blew around the Factory. In summer the winds lifted the dust and carried it, like a traveller on a dirty, frenetic roundabout, around the Factory. On winter days, like this one, the winds caught the snow flurries and drifted them on the down-wind side of the building.

Bill Payne had not been back there since the day it opened, six years ago. The outside of the building was now unfamiliar. He found it hard to remember where the Minister stood when he gave that stirring speech about firsts for Britain and new technology harnessed by man for man.

Bill announced himself at the door. The managing micro, programmed for security, took some time to read his smart card, link up with the national security computer and validate his voice pattern. He realised that he should have specified a series 3 not 2 when he drew up that part of the design. Eventually the door opened and he was admitted.

The lights were still flickering on as he walked in. They had not been used since the last regular check ten months before and they were cold. It struck him that it was as cold in here as it was outside. That should not be possible; he had worked out the amount of heat needed carefully. The walls had been thoroughly insulated and with small windows the heat of the robots would be enough to keep the building above 10°C even on the coldest of days. In summer the air-conditioning would take care of the heat when the Managing Micro requested it. That was the place to start — the Manager.

Environmental monitoring meant measuring the temperature and humidity of the building. This was done using around a hundred sensors placed around the Factory. They measured just two things — temperature and humidity. The Micro was programmed to look constantly at all of the sensors and if any readings were too high or too low, it kicked in the air conditioner and informed Head Office during its daily report. It was the absence of this message that had alerted Bill to the problems.

He moved to the computer room first of all and scanned the monitor screens above the computer. They were blank. He pressed BREAK and tried RESET A message appeared on the monitor.

'I/O modem units disconnected' Someone had tampered with this machine. It took Bill less than five minutes to unscrew the computer from its base and to find the connector that should have been firmly attached to the port. Not only was it disconnected, but it had been badly mauled. Yet whoever had done this had taken the trouble to screw the machine back down again.

As he put the micro back in its slot, the other screens suddenly came to life. What they were printing was garbage. Although the noise from the fans was unchanged a sudden chatter seemed to fill the room, as if the rubbish on the screen was caused by a crowd in the next room. Bill felt suddenly very alone and helpless. There was no way of knowing what was happening in the rest of the building. He decided that it was time to see for himself what was happening on the factory floor.

The floor area was out of bounds to normal maintenance engineers. They were not needed there since the machines were all self-maintaining. It was also a dangerous area. The robots had limited sensors fitted; sufficient for the jobs they were programmed for, but very little use beyond that. If anything got in their way at the wrong moment, say when they were turning and had switched out their sensors, then whatever it was got flattened. Bill had designed the floor and so knew it well.

Every twist and turn, each fixed machine and the paths of the mobile units he had worked out. He opened the door onto the work area with some difficulty. Something large had distorted the frame.

There was no danger; the machinery lay idle. As the lights settled down to their antiseptic glare and his eyes adjusted to the level, grotesque statues emerged from the gloom. Remote handling arms locked together; transporter pallets crashed into each other; a milling machine suspended by the overhead crane. Bill groaned. How could this have happened? Why did the fail-safe cut-outs not work? He had thought of everything, hadn't he?

Back to the computing room. Obviously someone had got in, disconnected the links to the outside and proceeded to play musical chairs with the robots. He broke into the Manager Micro and entered his password. The security log showed that no one had entered the building during the ten months between the engineer's call and his entry some thirty minutes ago. What had happened had been caused from inside. There must be an enormous bug in the programs controlling the Factory. That would be difficult to find. All he and his team had done was buy the software off-the-shelf. When it was run on this model of hardware it made the system intelligent and the application programs were written by the host computer. There was no easy way of finding the fault in this type of program. He would have to take a copy of the operating disc back to Head Office and debug it there. The Boss would not be happy. Their first completely automatic Factory broken down and held up for weeks while the fault was traced.

There was just one possibility. The series 2 could understand a limited number of spoken words provided the sentences were not too long. Bill decided to have a go.
'Who got into the Factory?'
'No one got into the Factory'
'Why have the machines stopped?'
'The machines are broken'
Bill nearly stopped there!
'Why did you not tell Head Office?'
'It was disconnected'

'Who disconnected you?'

'Programmable arms 20 and 21'

Bill sighed. It was as he feared: the machines had done it to themselves. What had made them do such a stupid thing?

'Why were arms 20 and 21 told to do this?'

'I was bored'

Bill had never thrown a chair through a monitor screen before. The sound of breaking glass was still echoing round the silent factory as he passed through the main door whistling tunelessly to himself.

Answer the following as fully as you can.

1 How many people worked in the Factory?

2 The Managing Micro seemed to do several jobs. What were the three given in the story?

3 What is a sensor?

4 How often was the Factory checked
(a) by phone?
(b) by visits?

5 The Factory was opened by a Minister. Why did someone so important open it?

6 The site of the Factory was bleak. What was the reason given in the story for the Factory being built there?

7 There was another reason for the choice of site that is not written down in the story but could be guessed. What do you think the reason is?

8 What steps were taken before Bill was allowed into the Factory?

9 Why was Bill, rather than anyone else, told to go to the Factory?

10 What heated the Factory?

11 What had the machines done before they stopped?

12 What information did the security log contain?

13 The software controlling the Factory had been bought 'off-the-shelf'. What does this mean?

14 Who or what wrote the control programs for the Factory?

15 What is a host computer?

16 What did **converse mode** allow Bill to do easily?

17 Why did the Managing Micro cause the machines to destroy each other?

18 Who do you think should pay for the damage?

19 Whom did the Factory benefit?

20 Who suffered because the Factory was built?

21 Who would have suffered if the Factory had not been built?

TOPICS FOR DISCUSSION

D1 Credit cards and smart cards are in use now. They make it easy to keep track of your own spending. They can also be used to trace your movements and to find out about your spending habits. How would you feel if they totally replaced the sort of money that we use today?

D2 When it becomes possible to link the human brain directly to computers how would you feel about having such a link implanted in your brain? What sort of advantages would it have? What would be the advantages and disadvantages of not having a link if your friends all had one?

D3 If the factory of the future is run by robots what sort of jobs have disappeared? What sort of work is left that cannot be done by machine?

D4 It has been said that people cannot tell the difference between technology and magic in a primitive society. Which uses of computers do you think would appear magical to a person who lived fifty years ago? What 'magical' uses do you think will be around in fifty years time?

The note

Someday you may have to write to a school explaining why your child is missing from lessons. Instead of the sort of letters written today you may have to write one like this:

To the Headprogrammer, Smallville School

Dear Teacher,

My son Jeremy will not be online today. He is ill and I blame the school for his illness. I know he needs that biolink thing on his scalp, but when we had him done I didn't know as it would make him into a different person. He used to be a normal boy, not perfect I know, but normal. I used to get in the odd bit of bother at school and so I know what it's like. He used to go out and play football with his mates. Then he had that thing fitted two years ago. Since then he's been stuck on it every night for three hours or more. I even caught him up at four o'clock one morning logged-on. When I ask what he's up to all I get is 'School work, Mum, go away'. Sometimes it's not as polite as that. I don't think it's always school work but mostly it is.

Anyway, last night he fell asleep over the keyboard, fell off the chair and knocked hisself out on the bedside table. The Doctor said he will be OK given a few days rest. I'll let him log on again next Monday.

What I want to know is this. Why does the school make him do so much work in his own time? If he doesn't get it done during school time why does he have to do it at all? I'm really fed up with this. If you don't do nothing about it I'm going to send him to a place that still uses pens and paper.

Yours upset

Mrs Davis (Mother)

EXERCISES

1 Why was Jeremy away from school?

2 What did he have fitted two years ago?

3 What did the biolink make possible?

4 What change did Mrs. Davis see in her son?

5 What is Mrs. Davis complaining about?

6 What does she threaten to do?

Glossary

amplifier   a device that increases the size of a signal.
analogue computer   a computer that uses continuously changing voltages and currents to model a system.
analogue – digital converter   a device that changes voltages or currents into numbers.
artificial intelligence   making computers behave like humans in the way they solve problems and make decisions.
backup   to copy data.
chips   the common name for the integrated electronic circuits which form the building blocks of computer design.
command   characters or groups of characters that tell a computer what to do.
computer   a machine that can be programmed to take in information, change the form of that information, and store it or send it out again.
cursor   the square, line or dot on a screen that shows where the next character will be printed.
data   another word for information.
database   a collection of information that can be dealt with by computer.
data processing   re-arranging information.
digital computer   a computer that processes numbers.
disc   see floppy disc.
documentation   the printed information that comes with a program giving instructions on how to use it.
electronic mail   messages sent by phone line or radio waves using computer.
electronic warfare   controlling weapons electronically.
expert system   a program that can provide expert advice.
feedback   a path in a system that sends information back to the start of the system for monitoring purposes.
field   part of a record which contains several characters.
file   a collection of records.
floppy disc   a plastic disc coated with magnetic material. It is used to store information permanently which can then be read back.
flow diagram   a picture of a process using different shaped boxes.
hacker   the name given to a criminal who tries to break into computer systems from the outside.
hardware   the pieces that make up a computer.
hybrid computer   a computer that uses both digital and analogue parts.
information   a collection of facts and figures.
information technology   the machinery that is used to re-arrange information.
input   to put data into a computer.
input device   the machine which sends data into a computer.
integrated circuit   a slice of semiconductor that has been 'etched' to make it into a system of sub-circuits.
interface   part of a computer system that links one part to another.
joystick   a lever mounted on a box which is attached to switches or potentiometers. It is an input device which can send commands to a computer.
key   the part of a record used to find it in a database.
keyboard   the key switches, arranged like those of a typewriter, which are commonly used to input information into a computer.
knowledge base   a collection of information about a particular topic.
light pen   An input device that can be used to interact directly with a computer screen.
load   to place information into the memory of a computer.
mailing list   a database containing names and addresses.
menu   a screen displaying the options a user can select in a program.
modem   MOdulator/DEModulator. A device that changes data so that it can be sent down a telephone line. It can also separate the data from the signal.
monitor   a high definition screen which looks like a TV.
network   A collection of computers all connected together.
output   to send data from a computer to another device.
peripheral   a device connected to a computer.
port   the electrical connections to other devices on the outside of a computer.
process   a collection of actions done by a computer.
program   a collection of commands that tells a computer what to do.
RAM (random access memory)   memory in which data can be written or read directly to one position without having to read or write other information first.
ROM (read only memory)   memory circuits that cannot be altered easily.
record   part of a file containing several fields.
robot   a machine that can do similar things to humans.
run   to set a program going.
save   to store information on tape or disc so that it can be used again.
screen   the part of a computer system that displays information. It is usually a cathode ray tube.
sector   part of a track on a disc.
simulator   a program or a device that behaves like some other system.
signal   an electrical voltage used to represent binary digits.
software   another word for program.
sort   to re-arrange information according to certain rules. An alphabetical sort would re-arrange information into alphabetic lists.
spreadsheet   a computer program that presents information as tables. It is used for planning a company or business.
system   a collection of interconnected devices.
track   the circular lines on a formatted disc.
transducer   a device that changes one type of energy into another.
user   someone who uses a computer to do a job.
utility   a program that is used to handle files.
validate   to check information before it is processed.
verify   to check that discs have been formatted correctly.
voice recognition   using the spoken word to send information to a computer.
word processing   using a computer to write, change, save and print documents.